AF471021

Merchant Ship
Design since 1945

LNG AQUARIUS

Merchant Ship Design since 1945

B. SMITH

LONDON

IAN ALLAN LTD

First published 1984

ISBN 0 7110 1348 9

All rights reserved. No part of this book may be reproduced or transmitted in any form or by any means, electronic or mechanical, including photo-copying, recording or by any information storage and retrieval system, without permission from the Publisher in writing.

© Ian Allan Ltd 1984

Published by Ian Allan Ltd, Shepperton, Surrey; and printed by Ian Allan Printing Ltd at their works at Coombelands in Runnymede, England.

Contents

Acknowledgements

While it is not possible to list the numerous sources of information that assisted the writing of this book, the author gratefully acknowledges such help, including the many companies mentioned in the various chapters. The following organisations are listed because of their particular cooperation in providing material and data, or else being outstanding and reliable sources of information: Appledore Shipbuilders Ltd; Atlantic Container Line (ACL); Ben Line; Blohm + Voss; Bonar Hugh Smith; British Hovercraft Corp Ltd; British Shipbuilders; British Telecom International; Cunard Line; Det Forande Dampskibs-Selskab (DFDS); Ferguson-Ailsa Ltd; Govan Shipbuilding Co Ltd; Ishikawajima-Harima Heavy Industries (IHI); Kawasaki Heavy Industries; Lloyd's Register of Shipping (Shipping Information Services Group); Marconi Marine Ltd; Mary Rose Trust; Mitsubishi Heavy Industries Ltd; Royal Institution of Naval Architects (The Institution's journal, *The Naval Architect*); Scott-Lithgow Ltd, Schottel-Werft; Sperry Marine Systems; Society of Naval Architects and Marine Engineers (Society's journal, *Marine Technology*); SS *Great Britain* Project; Sun Shipbuilding Corp; Townsend Thoresen.

The tanker fleets within the major oil companies of Shell, Esso and Amoco have also been of great assistance in providing photographic material while lastly, the author wishes to extend his appreciation and gratitude to colleague and naval architect John Barfoot for his assistance in researching and checking this work.

Abbreviations

ACV	Air cushioned vehicle
AFRA (MAX)	Average freight assessment (max)
ARPA	Automatic radar plotting aids
BCV	Barge carrying vessel
BHC	British Hovercraft Corp
BS	British Shipbuilders
BSRA	British Ship Research Association
CBM	Conventional buoy mooring
CNC	Computerised numerical control
CP	Controllable pitch
CPA	Closest point of approach
CSW	Chilled sea water
DP	Dynamic positioning
dwt	Deadweight measured in long tons unless specified as metric tonnes
EBCS	European Barge Carrier System
ELSBM	Exposed location single-point buoy mooring
flo/flo	Float-on/float-off
GEM	Ground effect machine
GRP	Glass-reinforced plastic
grt	Gross registered tonnage
IHI	Ishikawajima-Harima Heavy Industries
IMO	Inter-Government Maritime Organisation
ITB	Integrated tug barge
JPQS	Japanese shipbuilding quality standard
kts	Knots
LASH	Lighter aboard ship
LNG	Liquid natural gas
lo/lo	Lift-on/lift-off
LPG	Liquid petroleum gas
LSD	Landing ship dock
LST	Landing ship tank
NC	Numerically controlled
NDT	Non-destructive testing
nm	Nautical mile
OBO	Ore/bulk/oil
PCC	Pure car carrier
PPI	Planned position indicator
RDF	Radio direction finder
ro/ro	Roll-on/roll-off
RSW	Refrigerated sea water
SALM	Single anchor-leg mooring
SBM	SPAR buoy mooring
SES	Surface effect ship
SPBM	Single-point buoy mooring
STP	Special trade passenger
SWBM	Still water bending moment
TEU	Twenty-foot equivalent unit
TSPP	Tanker safety and pollution prevention
ULCC	Ultra-large crude carrier
VLBC	Very large bulk carrier
VLCC	Very large crude carrier

BENDORAN

Introduction

Man's fascination with sea travel extends right back to Egyptian times and before. During that early period marine transport evolved from primitive dug-outs to Athenian triremes. The propulsive mechanism was muscle power and oars, and later, sails. It took thousands of years to reach the stage of iron ships and steam power, and then only a few decades to see a complete transformation in sea transport.

The 19th and 20th centuries has seen more changes in ship design and construction than the whole of previous maritime history. Many of the radical changes have occurred since World War 2 and it is this period of marine development with which the present book deals. It is always useful to know the story behind the story, and this chapter provides a lead-up to this period.

Forms of water transport have been invented independently in many different parts of the world. Dug-out canoes similar to those in Europe thousands of years ago are still being made and used in Central Africa and New Guinea. Over the years these canoes were eventually fitted with outriggers and made more seaworthy to enable longer voyages. Chinese shipping led to such strange craft as 'crooked bow' and 'crooked stern' junks, and the developments from various cultures in early shipping eventually overlapped to create new trends. The Elizabethan galleon, Yorkshire coble and modern liner show the results of such specialised endeavours.

The beginning of 'northern' ships, like that of so many others, is lost in the mists of time, but Egypt appears to have constructed proper ships about 6,000 years ago. As the country lacked large trees the hulls were made of small irregularly shaped pieces of wood held together by dovetails, dowels or even stitching. There was no keel and the longitudinal strength was provided by ropes. For such vessels a heavy rope ran from bow to stern and was tightened by twisting it in the middle in order to resist the tendency toward hogging. From earliest recorded times the vessels were

Viking Ship.

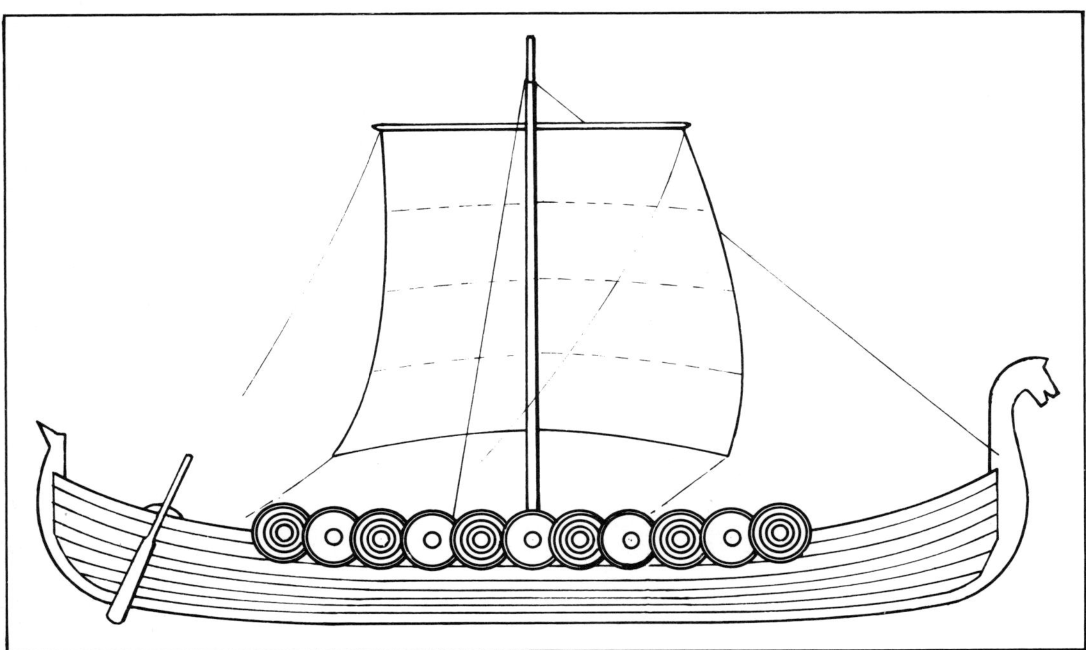

A contemporary representation of the *Mary Rose*.
The Mary Rose Trust

fitted with a square sail and the masts of larger ships could be lowered.

The Minoan civilisation, which properly began about 3,000BC, has left little record of its shipping activities but there are a few pictures of Phoenician ships (700BC) showing that by then oars working from fulcrum had replaced paddles. The Greek civilisation (which overlapped the Phoenician) offers more evidence of its shipping efforts through pictures on pottery. The construction methods were similar to modern techniques with a keel, frames and planks attached edge-to-edge (carvel construction). The Greek galley was a long narrow craft with two (bireme) or three (trireme) banks of oars, and like Egyptian vessels, equipped with a square sail and a mast that could be lowered. By 500BC larger craft were fitted with an outrigger, allowing for three banks of oars to be worked from a smaller space, an arrangement which lasted until the 18th century.

The Romans followed on from the Greeks. In their wars with Carthage they were beaten by the Carthaginians because the latter's sea power was greater. The Romans then copied their opponent's vessels plank for plank, and their war galleons had a platform from which they could board the enemy. Their trading vessels had more design features; their well-known grain ships had rounded hulls that relied entirely on sails.

Not many design changes occurred in the Mediterranean until the invention of the lateen sail, which properly originated in the Persian Gulf in 500AD. This triangular sail was the first to be set fore and aft. The typical ships of the Mediterranean at the start of the 16th century were the war and trading galleys. A galley was normally about 40m long and 5m in breadth, with 25 to 30 benches on each side and three oarsmen sitting on each bench. These galleys were still being used in the 18th century.

Northern people were still using dug-outs during the time of the Phoenicians, but by the late 8th century the Scandinavians had developed the famous Viking 'long ship'. This clinker (overlapping planks) built open vessel had a high bow and stern and was propelled by oars and a square sail. For many years this type of craft dominated northern waters; even William the Conqueror's ships were of the same design. A multitude of smaller craft, such as Hastings luggers and Brixham trawlers, was also being developed to suit particular jobs and districts. The larger craft evolved into the big ships.

War galleys in the area were adapted for trade, becoming wider in relation to keel length and thus allowing for more cargo space. They were single-masted square-rigged ships with castles built at the bow and stern during times of war. The steering equipment also changed over the years: first came the steering oar, then the side rudder, which was replaced by the stern rudder in the 13th century, making for a straighter stern. It was thus that the ubiquitous wooden galleons slowly evolved.

Permanent structures, sometimes overhanging the sides, had replaced the temporary castles by 1400AD, and the stern became rounder. By the mid-15th century

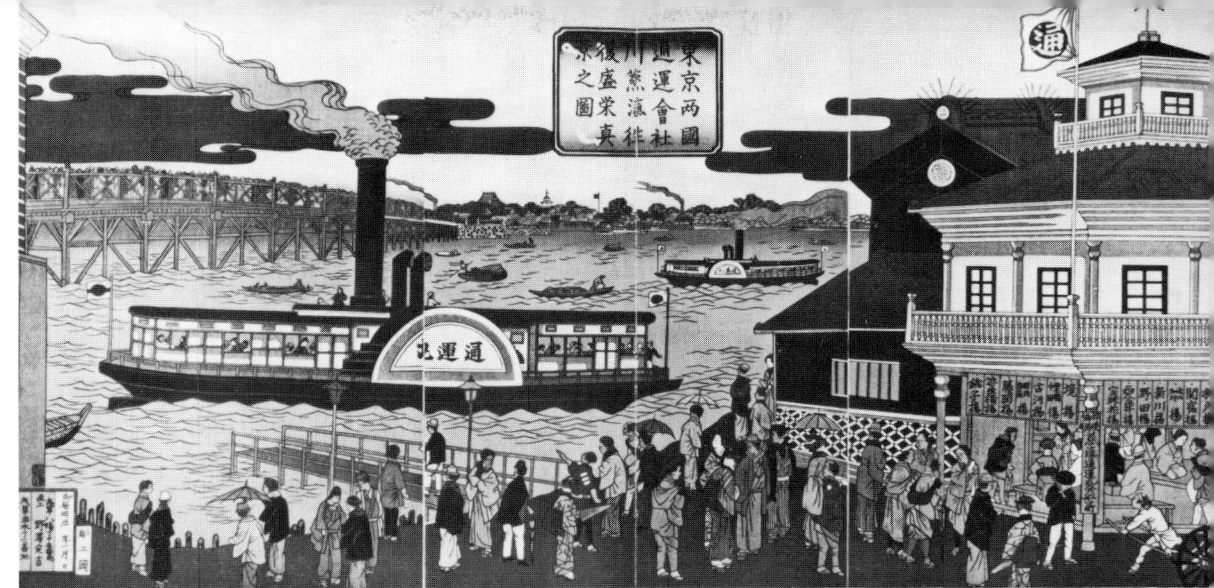

The *Tsu-un Maru*, the first merchant steam ship from a Japanese yard, completed by IHI in 1877. *IHI*

a small second (mizzen) mast had been added, on which was spread a lateen sail. The earliest picture of a three-masted ship can be seen on the seal of Louis Bourbon (1466), and other sails were added during the course of time. The *Louis de Bourbon* had a large mainmast, a foremast and a mizzen mast which had a lateen sail. This combination of sails made it possible to make use of almost every kind of wind. Able to carry stores and people, this ship also had a tiller with the rudder stock passing through the hull. The credit for designing and perfecting such new ships must go to the shipwrights of Spain, Portugal and Brittany.

In 1539 the rebuilt *Harry Grace à Dieu* was launched and in a contemporary picture it is shown with four masts. She is also famous for being the first English ship built as a man-of-war. The *Harry Grace à Dieu* weighed 1,000 tons and carried 21 heavy brass guns, 130 iron guns and a crew of 700. Royal Navy ships during that period were divided into four classes: ships, galleasses, pinnaces and barges. The ships had high castles, and galleasses lower castles and beakheads. Pinnaces were quite small and barges smaller still, each weighing only 20 tons and fitted with oars.

The Tudor ship most prominent in the public eye of today is the 700ton 91-gun carrick *Mary Rose*, a converted merchantman which capsized in 1545 just off Portsmouth before Henry VIII's eyes and was then found, still preserved in the silt, and salvaged in 1982. During Henry VIII's reign ships and guns were both improved and hulls, instead of being clinker-built, were made of carvel construction. Protection against shipworm was also introduced by sheathing hulls to shield from attack.

Designers were becoming conscious of 'shipshape' hull forms and a famous shipwright, Phineas Pett, produced in 1769 the *Sovereign of the Seas*, which had an underwater hull that curved up to well beyond the waterline. Her masts also carried a fourth sail up above called the 'royals', perhaps taken from her name. Changes were also taking place in steering: by 1720 the clumsy whipstaff had been replaced by the windlass, then almost immediately this was replaced by

SS *Great Britain* — the first iron ship built and the first ship to be fitted with a screw propeller. *SWPA*

The ill-fated *Titanic* leaving Southampton harbour.
National Maritime Museum

the wheel. Yet for all these changes and improvements the wooden ships barely reached 200ft in length; the largest wooden ship of all — the USS *Pennsylvania* — was a mere 210ft. From about 1800 onwards wooden ship design remained static, then the ever growing Industrial Revolution, carrying in its flood new techniques and ideas, swamped them out of existence. Wood and sails were superseded by iron and steam — but not before a final flurry of improvements to sailing trading ships, which led to the famous clipper ships, and their unparalleled performance.

Marine transport — fuelled by the Industrial Revolution — took a leap into the future in the mid-19th century. The harnessing of steam to machinery made sails redundant almost overnight. Ships-of-the-line became just floating memorials to great battles such as Trafalgar, and within a decade or so the long and magnificent era of the wooden ship had drawn to an end. Nelson's famous flagship, the *Victory*, now lies in drydock at Portsmouth Dockyard as a nostalgic reminder of those times.

Watt and Newcomen had made the steam engine successful, and other experimenters began applying it to ship drives. The Marquis Claude de Jouffray d'abbens in 1783 — plus a number of others at that time — had built experimental steamboats, but it was Robert Fuller who in 1807 launched the first successful steamboat, the *Claremont*. Then in 1819 the auxiliary-powered *Savannah* crossed the Atlantic, powered by steam a small part of the way.

The one disadvantage of such craft in those early days was their high fuel consumption, which made ocean crossings impossible. The engines then were low-pressure jet-condensing units, but in 1834 Samuel

Hall patented the 'surface' condenser which, along with rising boiler pressures, improved economy and made ocean voyages possible. The *Sirius* in 1838, followed by the *Great Western*, were able to steam right across the Atlantic, and the era of steam had dawned.

The next important step to be taken was the construction of iron hulls. In 1843 the famous engineer Isambard Kingdom Brunel designed the first iron ship, the *Great Britain*. This ship also incorporated a remarkable innovation in marine propulsion — it was fitted with a screw propeller. The marine screw can be attributed to no single inventor; John Ericsson and Francis Pettit Smit both had a share in it and later, John Penn invented the Lignum Vitae-lined sternbush. The *Great Britain* was the first vessel to cross the Atlantic solely by propeller, and in 1858 Brunel built the *Great Eastern*, but this underpowered vessel was not a commercial success, although it did lay the first underwater cable.

Iron was soon displaced by a new material — mild steel. This was brought about by work from Bessemer and others in the late 1850s. Mild steel is still used today as the most common material in shipbuilding, and its use in those days resulted in an increase in ship sizes. Powerplant design was also improving, bringing about the 'compound' engine which resulted in much improved economy. This, combined with twin screws, finally rang the death knell to sail; ships could now steam across the oceans with confidence and assurance.

From 1870 onwards detailed improvements were made; boiler pressures, triple, then quadruple engines and so on. They were all heralding the next major step in marine design — the steam turbine. The stage was set in 1897 at the great Naval Review at Spithead. It was then that this innovative power mechanism was introduced. The first turbine-engined ship — the famous launch *Turbina* — steamed past the rest of the fleet at a previously unheard of speed of over 30kts to the dumbfoundment of brass hats and sailors alike. Charles Parsons — later Sir Charles — had achieved this major breakthrough on his own, but many others followed his lead.

Eight years later the 30,000-ton *Mauretania* — powered by quadruple turbines giving 70,000hp — was designed to cross the Atlantic at a speed of 25kts. Later saw the entry of the diesel engine for smaller ships. Developed by Rudolph Diesel and others, this compression-ignition engine, burning heavy oil, went to sea in 1921.

The sinking of the supposedly unsinkable British White Star liner *Titanic* in 1912 made the marine world safety conscious. Over 1,500 people lost their lives after it had struck an iceberg, and the resulting enquiry found there were not enough lifeboats on board to cater for the ship's total complement. Nevertheless, this tragedy did not stop other great liners such as the *Queen Mary* and *Queen Elizabeth* from being built. But the era of the luxury liner was drawing to a close; indeed, World War 2 was to change many things, including shipbuilding trends and marine transport. The postwar era brought about as many radical changes in the marine world as those of the 19th century. This book is devoted to that part of the long and prestigious history of man's fascination with the sea.

The luxury liner *Queen Mary*, probably the most famous of all the 'Queens'. *Real Photographs*

1
World Shipbuilding and Shipyards

World shipbuilding has gone through a series of booms and slumps since the end of World War 2. A number of nations have completely reorganised and modernised their shipyards during this period, some because of the ruins brought about by the conflict, and others because of planned economic programmes. New leaders have emerged in this postwar era — a prime example being Japan — while other countries such as Britain, which for decades not only ruled the waves but shipping and ship construction, have declined in the international maritime league. This chapter, in giving a brief global review of shipbuilding and shipyards since World War 2, does not claim to present a complete and in-depth picture of a very complex subject but merely highlight some important trends and developments in major areas and countries.

In 1978 the world's fleet reached a peak of 406 million gross tons, and then came a slump that was the worst since the early 1930s. With gloomy forecasts predicting that the decline would continue, shipbuilding output was at its lowest for 12 years in 1979, but by 1980 there were signs of recovery, although that same year the world shipping industry was described as in real crisis, where too much tonnage was chasing too little traffic. In 1982 Lloyd's Register of Shipping in its annual report released in March of that year, recorded a dramatic improvement in shipbuilding work, although the chairman of Lloyd's Register of Shipping reviewed the future less optimistically.

Some significant trends in the worldwide shipbuilding scene in postwar years have seen increasing state-ownership and nationalisation of shipbuilding industries, together with the modernisation and

An aerial view of Scott Lithgow's shipyard prior to nationalisation. *Scott Lithgow*

Upriver view from the air of Govan Shipbuilders' yard on the Clyde, showing the three building berths ranged alongside the module hall and the outfitting basin. *Govan Shipbuilders*

specialisation of facilities. Developing countries are beginning to make their presence felt in the marine market, while other nations have leapt from obscurity to prominence. Automated procedures and mass assembly techniques have come to dominate construction, while the design side relies ever more on computer technology and the generation of standard designs for particular ship types.

Europe has seen two major conflicts in the first half of this century, with victory in both cases relying as much on sea transportation and blockade as with guns and tanks. Britain's blockade of German sea trade in the world wars, and its ability to maintain imports by means of the convoy system, immensely aided the victory bells to chime. After World War 2 the European shipbuilding scene was to alter radically in organisation and technology, resulting in greater efficiency and competitiveness.

Britain

British shipbuilding had boom periods in the 1940s and 1950s then had to face increasing worldwide competition, including that from Japan. There followed a number of reports to try to meet the challenge, including the Geddes Report of 1966 which recommended the rationalisation of the industry into four big and compact groups. Following this came legislation by Parliament in the form of the Shipbuilding Industry Act, 1967, to implement the Geddes Report recommendations. The Act established the Shipbuilding Industry Board and that year the industry underwent a major reorganisation, 27 companies being reduced to 11. Then in 1975 the government conducted a technological survey of all UK yards in connection with the nationalisation of the industry, an event which was implemented in July 1977. The nationalised industry, British Shipbuilders, took under its umbrella 30 companies, embracing 90 subsidiaries, engaged in new construction, marine engineering and repair.

Today, British Shipbuilders (BS) is organised into five divisions, namely Merchant Shipbuilding, Warshipbuilding, Engineering, Shiprepair and Offshore. Its large merchant shipbuilding division comprises Austin & Pickersgill Ltd, Govan Shipbuilders Ltd, Smith's Dock Ltd and Sunderland Shipbuilders Ltd, with Swan Hunter's as a composite yard, while its small merchant shipbuilding division has Appledore Shipbuilders Ltd, Ferguson-Ailsa Ltd, Clelands Shipbuilders Ltd, Goole Shipbuilders Ltd, Hall Russell Ltd and Henry Robb Ltd. The Offshore Division is represented by Cammell Laird, V.O. Offshore and Scott Lithgow, the last representing a group of companies, one being Scott Engineering, the oldest shipbuilding company in the world. These companies build a variety of vessels, including a family of designs. In the process of reorganisation the British shipbuilding industry workforce has been slimmed down from about 85,000 to 67,000 employees.

In the five years before nationalisation 14 British yards had been closed for various reasons. At that time virtually every country in the world had increased its tonnage except the UK. Despite substantial orders being received in the following years, Britain had slipped to 11th place in the world order book league by 1980. Recently, the marketing of standard ships by BS

was being consolidated into families of designs, the BS design team bringing together 14 existing yard designs and another 21 designs spanning a variety of ship types. These excellent and popular designs, together with a contracted and efficient industry, show every indication that the UK will once again be in the forefront of the maritime market.

One innovation introduced into British shipyards is the building of covered facilities and ship factories. Appledore Shipbuilders, North Devon, built the world's first ship factory which was completed in 1970 on a green field site, being planned from the beginning for efficient production uninterrupted by weather conditions. The factory can build pairs of ships up to 8,000 dwt. In 1975 Cammel Laird's shipyard at Birkenhead had installed a covered facility as part of a major reconstruction project. The whole yard was centred round a new construction hall where two ships — one of up to 135,000 dwt and the other of 85,000 dwt — could be constructed simultaneously under cover. A major project in the modernisation scheme for three shipyards owned by Sunderland Shipbuilders was the completion in 1976 of a new covered shipbuilding factory on the site of Doxford's old Pallion shipyard on the River Wear. This new facility was modelled on the Appledore yard and is capable of constructing two ships up to 35,000 dwt each, side by side. Yet another British merchant shipyard innovation is the new glass reinforced plastic (GRP) construction complex for Yarrow Shipbuilders, which was opened in 1979, although Vosper Thorneycroft had previously built such a facility for naval work in 1972.

East Germany

The shipbuilding industry of the German Democratic Republic was founded in 1949, like the country itself. At that time the country was only capable of building small fishing vessels: today it is one of the major shipbuilding countries in the world. This country — which

View of the world's first totally enclosed ship factory, built in 1970 on a green field site at Appledore, North Devon for Appledore Shipbuilders Ltd. *Appledore*

was born out of the ruins of World War 2 — concentrated on the series production of smaller and specialised ship types, the USSR being its major customer. Such concentration enabled flow-line production systems and a high concentration of prefabrication and other preparatory work to be done under cover. In 1979 the industry took a major step in development with the establishment on 1 January of a completely integrated shipbuilding industry combining under the name VEB Kombinet Schiffbau.

Italy

The Italian government has a substantial interest in shipbuilding and repair, as well as marine engineering, and as much as 85% of the industry is said to be owned by Fincantieri, an arm of the mammoth Institute for Industrial Reconstruction (IRI). Largest of all the shipyard complexes under Fincantieri's wing — and the largest group in the country — is Italcantieri SpA, with yards at Genoa, Sestri, Monfalcone (just outside Trieste) and at Castellammare di Stabia, not far from Naples. The Monfalcone shipyard — the largest in Italy — was modernised in the mid-1970s and geared to the series production of very large crude carriers (VLCCs).

Malta

Malta was once the Mediterranean home of the Royal Navy, whose base was the Grand Harbour. The island gained its independence in 1959 and the facilities round Malta Docks were changed over to commercial work, with naval activities run down. The drydocks were nationalised in 1968 and later extensively enlarged and expanded to encompass new shipbuilding work. Along with this surge into commercial shipbuild-

13

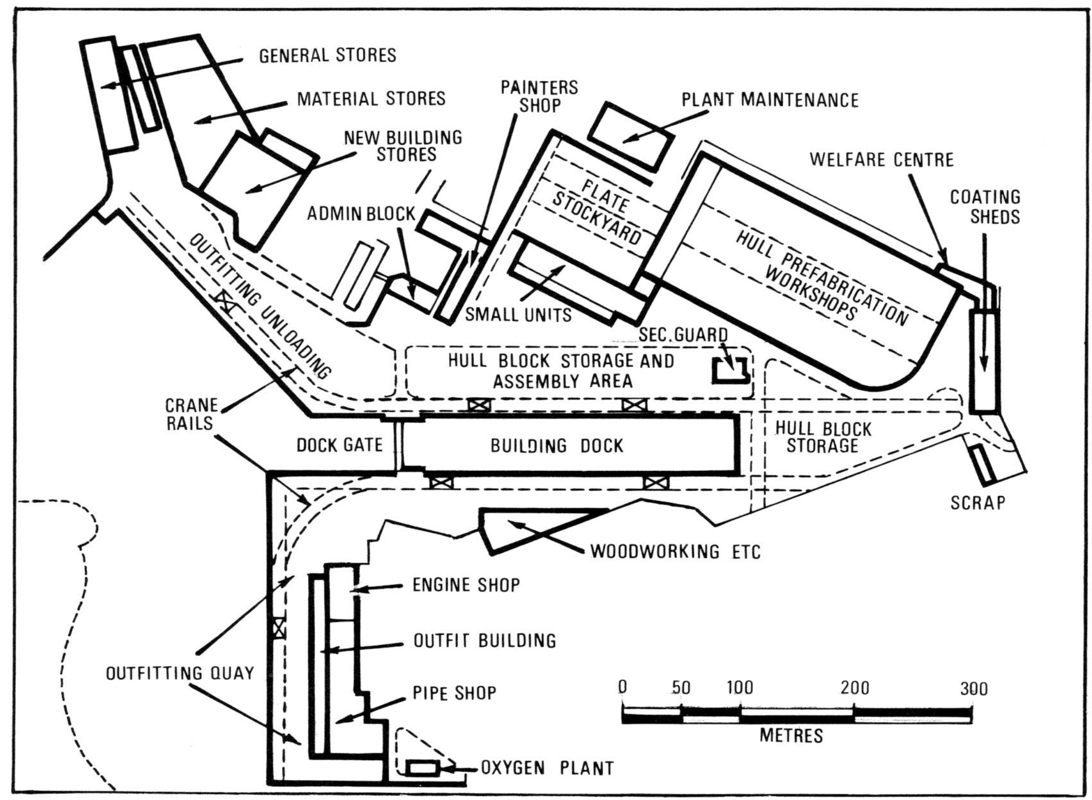

Planned layout of the Malta Shipbuilding Co's Marsa Shipyard.

ing was the start of construction of a new shipyard in 1980 at Marsa.

Scandinavia

Scandinavia has always been considered by shipowners to be a major area of world shipbuilding. Norway's shipyards are very versatile, being able to build anything from a 37m purse seiner to a 285,000 dwt supertanker. Moss Rosenberg Verft AS is one of Norway's largest shipbuilders, best known for its LNG carriers. The company operates two yards, one at Moss and the larger one at Rosenberg. Swedish shipbuilding is now under the government, with the last private shipbuilder, Kockums AB, becoming a member of the state-owned shipbuilding company, Svenska Varv, in 1979, despite company resistance. Kockums has a yard at Malmo which is one of the largest and most modern in Europe, and the company's final accedance to nationalisation was because of financial difficulties. The Soviet Union has always been a good customer of the Finnish shipbuilding industry, which specialises in icebreaking vessels and is a world leader in the design and construction of ferries and cruise liners. Altogether, Scandinavian shipbuilding regularly maintains a fair share of the world's shipbuilding trade.

Poland

Polish shipyards were reconstructed from the rubble of World War 2 but by 1976 had reached 12th position in the world shipbuilding league. United Polish Shipyards (UPS), with its headquarters at Gdansk, is an integrated organisation controlling research, technical, productive and economic aspects of Polish shipbuilding and marketing. It has three major shipyards for constructing ocean-going ships; on the Baltic coast at Gdansk, Gydnia and Szczecin. They started production between 1948 and 1951, and have since been modernised.

Other European Countries

Other European countries such as France, Spain and the German Federal Republic have made their contributions to the European shipbuilding scene, some being more successful than others. For instance, Spain's first custom-built shipyard for building liquefied gas carriers, launched in 1972, had run into trouble by 1978. West Germany has developed an efficient and competitive shipbuilding industry which has captured many orders over the years. Blohm+Voss is somewhat typical of the resurrection of that country's shipbuilding industry since World War 2. The company started business in 1877 and was active in the building of commercial and naval vessels during, and between the wars, including the launching of the battleship *Bismark* in 1939. In 1948 the shipyard began to be dismantled by the occupying powers but in 1954 permission was granted to build sea-going ships. From then on the company rapidly returned to its prewar status as a major German shipbuilder.

Middle East

While European countries were trying to re-establish their shipbuilding industries after the holocaust of World War 2, developing countries were seeking to found their own industries, including shipbuilding; and one such area was the Middle East. The Middle East has constantly hit the headlines in recent years, either because of oil price rises that adversely affected the western economy or through military and political unrest. This sandy area of the globe produces more than half the world's crude and contains a similar proportion of reserves under its barren wastes. This factor, combined with the Arab-Israeli conflict, makes it a highly sensitive area in political and economic terms. Nevertheless, the petro-money that has poured into the area has produced rapid developments which include the creation of an indigenous shipbuilding industry to support its oil trade. In fact, efforts in this direction have made the Middle East a serious participant in the marine market.

It was in the Arabian Gulf that the world's largest ship repair complex was built, with three VLCC drydocks at Dubai, a half-million dwt dock at Bahrein and a 36,000 dwt floating dock at Kuwait. The dock at the Arab Ship Repair Yard (ASRY), Bahrein, went into service in October of 1977 when it docked its first VLCC. The Bandar complex in Iran can accommodate ships of up to a potential of one million tonnes dwt, while many smaller companies have expanded their facilities.

North America

Shipbuilding interest on the American continent has for a long time rested with the USA and Canada. The Canadians have a long and sound shipbuilding tradition, with companies such as the Davey Shipbuilding Company, Quebec, and Halifax Shipyards, Nova Scotia, producing large and small vessels for the domestic and foreign market. Now, Dome Petroleum's assessment for recovering hydrocarbons and other energy-related resources from the Canadian Beaufort Sea has initiated a study for a major new shipyard in that country.

The United States in past years has made great strides in marine mass assembly techniques and welding technology, starting with the famous Liberty ships of World War 2. When hostilities ceased it had the largest shipbuilding industry in the whole world but during the past 30 years this has contracted to a fraction of its former size due to loss of competitiveness. In recent years efforts have been made to rectify the situation and the Maritime Administration (MarAd) initiated the National Shipbuilding and Research Programme which, since 1971, has sponsored and jointly founded many research and development projects. A survey to improve American shipbuilding techniques in 1978 looked at some of the country's largest shipyards, which include Sun Shipbuilding, Chester, Pennsylvania, General Dynamics, Quincy, Massachusetts, and

A gas chemical carrier under construction at the Moss yard of Rosenberg Werft A/S, one of Norway's largest shipbuilders and best known for its construction of LNG carriers. *Kvaerner-group*

Aerial photograph of the Blohm + Voss shipyard in Hamburg, West Germany. The company typifies the recovery and worldwide success of German shipbuilding since World War 2. *Blohm + Voss*

An aerial view of the Sun Shipbuilding yard in Chester, Pennsylvania, USA. *Sun Shipbuilding*

Charleston, South Carolina, Todd Shipyards in California and Seattle, Washington, and Bethlehem Steel, Sparrows Point, Maryland. The survey came up with a number of proposals to make the industry more competitive in the world market, and since then it has been supported by large government subsidies, although few yards seem likely to remain viable. Naval work appears brighter, especially as the Reagan administration is committed to increasing naval expenditure.

South America

The South American countries have become more maritime conscious in postwar years and offshore exploration and development in that area has probably helped to stimulate such interest. Brazil is one of the leaders in the marine construction effort, yet its shipyards — founded in the last century — struggled through the 1950s until the government launched a development programme which in the late 1960s began to take effect. By 1976 it was seventh in the world order book and was going ahead with an expansion programme to put it even further ahead in international competition. Best known of all the Brazilian shipyards is the Manua yard, while some of the largest shipbuilding facilities are situated at the Inhauma Shipyard. The ISHIBRAS (Ishikawajima do Brasil Estaleiros SA) shipyard at Rio de Janeiro is considered one of the largest and most up-to-date ship-

The Ishibras shipyard in Brazil was established at Rio de Janeiro in 1959 as a joint venture between the Brazilian government and Japanese shipbuilders IHI. It is the largest and one of the most up to date shipyards in Latin America. *IHI*

yards in Latin America and was established in 1959 as a joint venture between the Japanese shipbuilder IHI and the Brazilian government. Among other new constructions, SD14s (Austin & Pickersgill's popular and successful standard design) have been built under licence in Brazil.

In Mexico production started in 1982 at the new Veracruz shipbuilding complex, which forms part of the Mexican government's current industrial development plan. Initially, production is directed toward product tankers in the 38-44,000 tonnes dwt range for Pemex, the state-owned national oil company, but it is also designed to enable the flexible manufacture of vessels up to Panama size and a variety of types up to 80,000 dwt.

Philippines

Further away in the Pacific is one of the world's newest yards, PNOC Marine Corporation's shipbuilding and ship repair complex at Baun on Batangas Bay south of Manila, Philippines. This yard has a hydraulic chain jack elevator and a hydraulic wheeled transfer system, one of the new and improved methods for transferring and launching ships. Such methods make possible significant savings in initial installation, repair and maintenance costs.

Far East

Finally, there is the Far East to consider in this postwar period of merchant ship development, and it is there that has been seen the most dramatic changes. These changes have occurred not only on the maritime scene, but also in other industrial areas and in the advance of trade. In the early part of this century the Far East was still largely an underdeveloped region, locked in ancient practices and ruled by feudal systems. Trade between the East and West was limited and difficult to establish. It was the oil companies such as Esso who helped prise open the lid off the eastern treasure chest, supplying kerosene for Chinese lamps. World War 2 and its political aftermath finally forced Asian countries into technological development and thrust them properly into the 20th century. There emerged from this pressurised evolution a surprising leader in the maritime field — Japan.

Before exploring the Japanese phenomenon some other Far Eastern maritime endeavours should be mentioned. Singapore has always been active in the shipping and shipbuilding world and another IHI joint venture — this time with the Singapore government — brought about the establishment in 1963 of the Jurong shipyard for the purpose of repairing large ships operating between the Arabian Gulf and Japan. Malaysia completed a shipyard at Labaun, an island off the coast of Sabah, East Malaysia, in 1982. The yard is owned by Sabah Shipbuilding Repairing and Engineering Sdn Bhd (SSRE) and includes some very advanced shipbuilding and repair facilities to cater for vessels up to 20,000 dwt. It is the largest covered shipyard in Malaysia. One of the meteoric rises in international shipbuilding has been that of South Korea. The country's activities in this field now seriously affects British and European yards, having emerged from obscurity to capture about 2% of the world's production. In 1978 it had reached the top 10 in the world's order book league, and the OKPO shipyard in South Korea is probably the largest in

IHI is the world's largest shipbuilder with six shipyards in Japan — Tokyo (*top*), Yokohama, Nagoya, Chita, Aioi (*bottom*) and Kwe. *IHI*

the world, being equipped with advanced and sophisticated machinery. But it is Japan that has been prominent in international shipbuilding in all its aspects since 1945, and this country's maritime efforts will quite rightly conclude this chapter.

An astonishing advance was made in Japanese shipbuilding in the decade just after World War 2. The Suez crisis created an increased worldwide demand for larger tankers and other vessels and during this period several Japanese yards were enlarged and modernised to meet the demand for construction. Some completely new yards were also built. Ship designs were standardised and modern management techniques introduced. By 1974 there were 31 major shipyards; 10 in Eastern Japan, 11 in the central region and 10 in the western districts. Among the largest of these shipbuilding companies are Ishikawajima-Harima Heavy Industries (IHI), previously mentioned in this chapter and the world's largest shipbuilder, owning six shipyards, Kawasaki Heavy Industries, and Mitsubishi Heavy Industries. IHI in particular has achieved many world shipbuilding records. Founded in 1853, the company built the *Tsu-un-Maru*, the first merchant ship from a Japanese private shipyard. After World War 2 it produced a series of world firsts in large tanker construction, beginning with a string of vessels under 150,000 dwt then building the first 150,000 dwt

VLCC, *Tokyo Maru*, in 1966. Following this came the first 480,000 dwt ULCC, the *Globtik Tokyo*, in 1973. The company's six shipyards are located in the major industrial zones of Japan and include the Kure shipyard which has a 400,000 and 800,000-ton large building block.

During all these postwar years Japanese shipyards advanced their ship construction technology. By 1950 the so-called 'block system' — where ships are built by assembling welded modules — was established. In the early 1950s the Japanese shipbuilding industry was busily adopting American welding technology and by the end of the decade Japanese-developed welding technologies began to appear. The 1960s saw this construction technology advance at full speed, and the impetus continued into the 1970s and beyond.

Among the initiators of this extraordinary Japanese shipbuilding development — which has produced some of the largest and most diverse ships ever built — is the Research Committee on Steel Shipbuilding in the Society of Naval Architects of Japan, and the Shipbuilding Division of the Welding Procedure Subcommittee in the Japanese Welding Engineering Society, both inaugurated soon after World War 2. To establish quality standards the professional societies inaugurated the Japanese Shipbuilding Quality Standard (JSQS) in 1966.

2
Shipyard Materials, Construction, Plant and Machinery

The basic element in any product is the raw material used, and for ships this is mainly steel. Shipbuilding steels start with the smelting of iron ore to make pig iron. This is usually done in a blast furnace and the resultant pig iron is 92-97% iron, the remainder being carbon, silicon manganese, sulphur and phosphorus. Subsequent steel manufacture refines the pig iron, ie reduces the impurities.

A steel may broadly be considered as an alloy of iron and carbon with percentages varying from about 0.1% carbon for mild steel to about 1.8% for some hardened steels. Steel for hull construction is usually mild steel containing 0.15 to 0.23% carbon and a reasonably high manganese content. This may be produced from one of four different processes; the open hearth process, the Bessemer converter process, the electric process or an oxygen process. The Bessemer process is not used for shipbuilding steels.

Ship classification societies originally had varying specifications but in 1959 the major societies agreed to standardise their requirements in order to reduce the required grades of steel to a minimum. There are now five different qualities of steel employed in merchant ship construction, graded A to E. Grades A and B are ordinary mild steels, the former being to Lloyd's Register requirements (and generally used in this country), while Grade B is to that of the American Bureau of Shipping (ABS). Grades C, D and E possess high notch-tough characteristics. (The toughness of a material is its ability to absorb energy before fracture and is related to its impact strength. A brittle material will have low toughness. Notch toughness is the energy required to break standard specimens in impact tests.)

Higher strength steels are often employed in the more highly stressed regions of large tankers and bulk carriers, and may also be supplied for use in constructing masts and rigging fittings where a reduction in scantlings is desirable. Use of higher strength steels

Module building has been one of the technical innovations in shipyard construction since 1945. This double bottom unit at Govan's shipyard is having ancillary equipment installed prior to being raised and placed in position on the berth.
Govan Shipbuilders

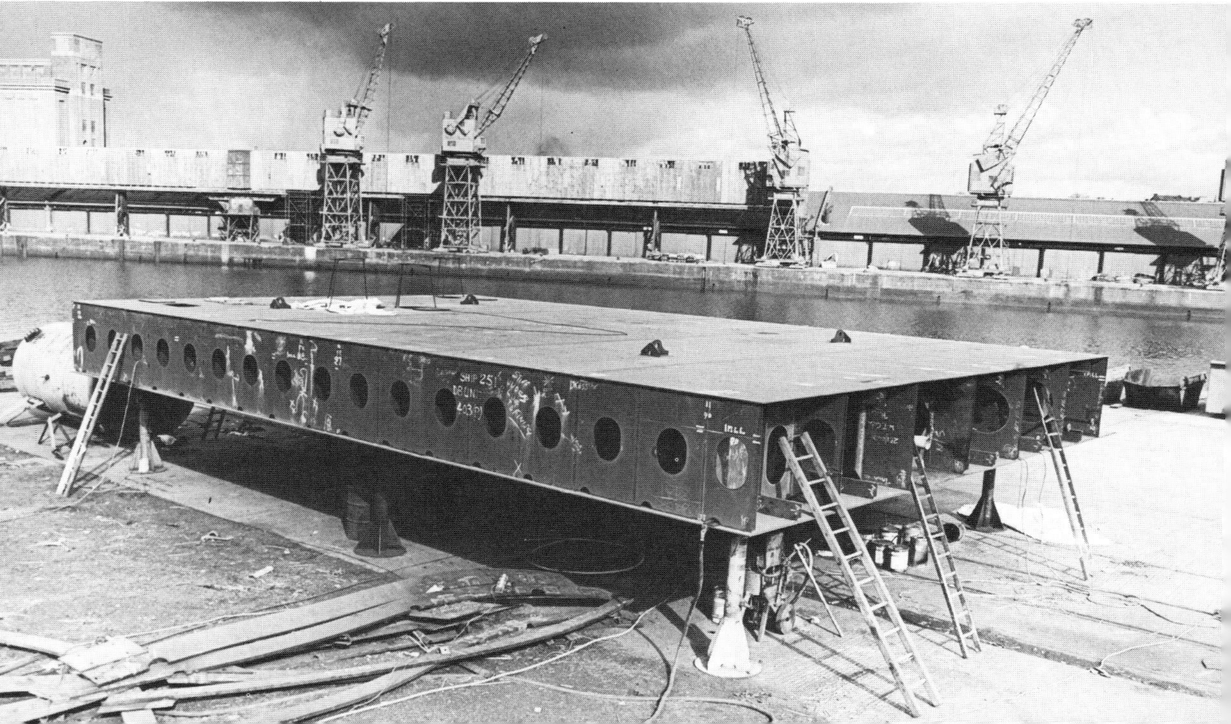

allows for reduction in thickness of deck, bottom, shell and framing, where fitted in the midship portion of larger vessels.

Aluminium alloys have only been used extensively in smaller ships, although aluminium superstructures have been constructed for larger vessels. This has resulted in a reduction of displacement and improved transverse stability.

Aluminium production at the present time means the mining of the ore Bauxite, which contains roughly 56% aluminium. Extracting the aluminium — which is a complicated and expensive process — involves two stages; the Bauxite is first purified to obtain pure aluminium oxide known as alumina, then the alumina is reduced to aluminium. Alloys are added where required before the metal is cast in billets or slabs for subsequent rolling, extrusion or other forming operations. Two distinct groups of aluminium alloys are now in use; non-heat treated alloys and heat treated alloys. Non-heat treated alloys are mainly used in Britain for ship structural purposes, and for such purposes those alloys with magnesium contents ranging from 3 to 5% are commonly used.

In the past 20-25 years reinforced plastics have made phenomenal advances as materials for pleasure boat and small craft construction. The Royal Navy has built mine countermeasures vessels of glass reinforced plastic (GRP) construction, while numerous smaller vessels have been built of single-skin GRP. The first GRP trawlers were built in South Africa in 1960 and Japan has used this material for fishing vessels since the early 1960s. Whether larger ships will be built in GRP or any other plastic is still a debatable point. Research and experience is still required on GRP connections for fabricated units, which would be the only practical and commercial approach to building really large vessels.

The construction of ships in the postwar era has undergone radical development. Where once the hull was built at a slipway with the keel laid first, followed by a long and tedious erection of bulkheads, frames and hull plating, the concept of modules or blocks, flowline processes and mass assembly techniques have greatly modified this piecemeal approach. Shipyard machinery has also developed to meet the demands of these new techniques, becoming more powerful and sophisticated.

Beginning at the design stage, the cumbersome hydrostatic and hydrodynamic calculations that were once part of initial and final design have now given way to computer programmes. Another feature of present day naval architecture — as in other engineering disciplines — is the increasing use of statistics to aid design. Component statistical analysis is an accepted technique in the general engineering industry as an aid to shop floor layout and production system design, and the ship hull component classification system was designed some years ago to allow for such an exercise to be carried out in shipbuilding. Computer-aided draughting systems have also evolved, such as the Datagrid II, a system that can interface with peripheral devices for programme and file storage as well as main-frame computers.

Other developments affect traditional mould loft techniques. The mould loft in a shipyard was until quite

Construction of ships is now a streamlined and computerised operation, resulting in complete hull sections already fitted with pipework and machinery arriving at the berth ready for fitting into place, as illustrated here. *Govan Shipbuilding*

recently a large wooden floor area for laying off details full size. This still applies for certain smaller or less progressive yards, but modern developments are directed towards reducing the amount of space required for mould loft work and eliminating some of the intermediate work where possible. From these full-scale lines a screive board would then be prepared where every fifth frame and intermediate frames were 'sighted' in, along with other information. These lines were 'screived' into the board by a special knife.

Plates marked by the traditional method require the preparation of wooden templates; this skill is very slow and takes up a lot of floor space. In the late 1950s, the $\frac{1}{10}$ scale or lofting system was introduced and has been widely adopted. This system consists of a drawing office fitted with a drawing board and a special long bench on which the lines may be faired, initially at 1/10 full size if a computer is not used for this purpose. The screive board will be a sheet of plywood or aluminium painted white. Different template drawings are made for operating a frame profiling machine than those that are required for use with an optical projection tower.

An optical projection tower is tailor-made for a site and has a marking table located at its base. An image from a 1/10 scale drawing, incorporated in a negative at 1/100 full size, is correctly positioned on a plate from a projection room in the tower. The plate is then marked with chalk lines and 'popped' with a centrepunch to record the lines. The 1/10 scale drawing should have thinner lines than those required for a profiler drawing.

An alternative to the above method — developed and used in Japan for marking plates — is the electro-print marking (EPM) process. This process eliminates hand marking but is used in association with manual flame cutting. The principle is as follows: first, photosensitive powder is sprinkled on the steel plate with a dusting device and is negatively charged either during or after the sprinkling process. The sprinkled powder sticks firmly to the surface of the steel plate electrostatically and the original drawing is then

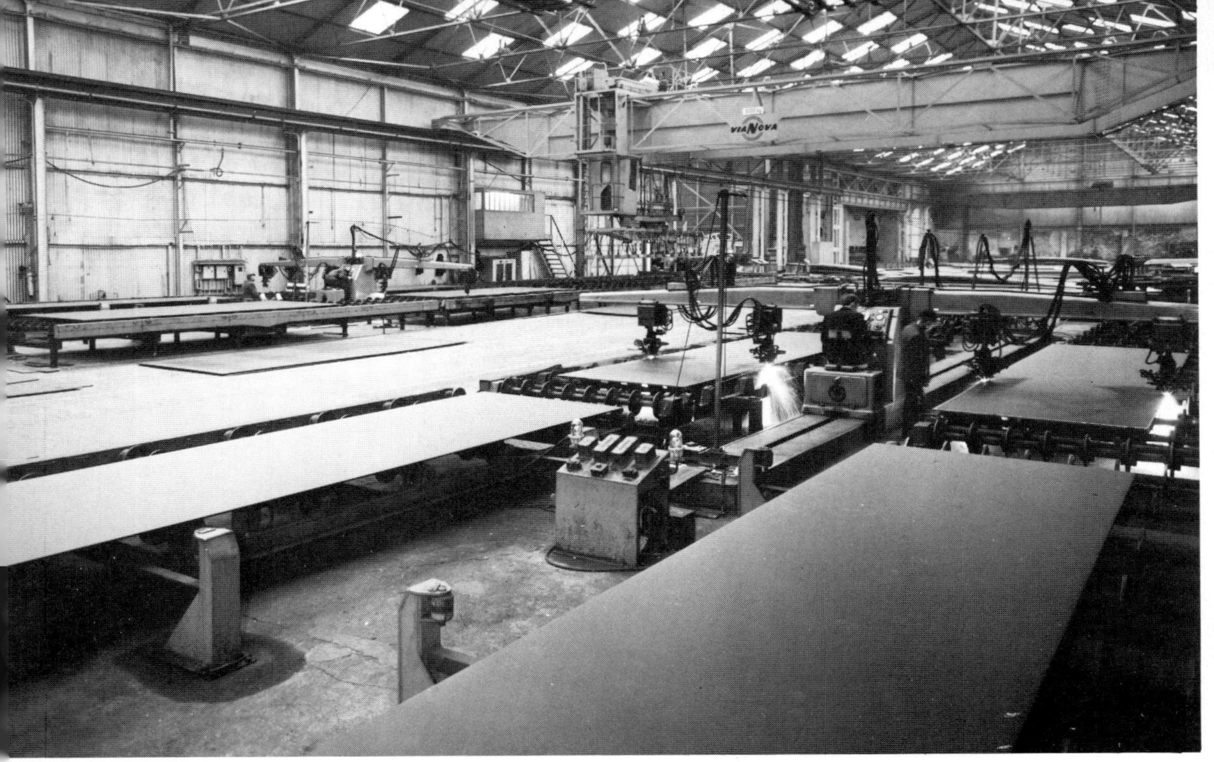

Plates undergoing cutting and edge preparation.
Scott Lithgow

projected on to the coated surface on an enlarged scale. Light exposure of the photo-sensitive powder results in a loss of electric charge. Air is blown on to the surface of plate to remove those portions of powder which have lost this charge. The remaining image is sprayed with a solvent to preserve contours.

Plates in a shipyard are now stacked horizontally, where it was once common practice to store them vertically in racks. Sections are also laid horizontally in convenient batches. To improve handling facilities in a stockyard a device known as a 'Captivator' is now available. It is really a conveyor on wheels with a magnetic pick-up and is capable of lifting the plates off a stack and hauling them on to the conveyor run-in to the plate shop, from which the Captivator can be remotely controlled.

Steel plates in transit from the steel mill to the shipyard are apt to get distorted, and plate straightening rolls known as 'mangles' are used to correct this. Modern mangles have to be capable of high output and are usually hydraulically powered and electrically controlled.

For handling plates, sections and fabricated units in a workshop there are gantries and cranes of various types, including a recently developed remote-controlled crane beam, 8m long and fitted with six pulleys, which reduces manual operations and enhances safety.

The postwar years have seen rapid development in the modular construction of ships and along with this has been a development in shipyard lifting and handling facilities at the building dock or berth. Giant overhead and floating cranes have evolved, as well as a number of other lifting and handling devices, both fixed and mobile. One example is the 1,200-ton capacity Goliath crane. One such crane is installed at the Quincy yard of General Dynamics, USA, and is reckoned to be one of the largest in the Western World. It is 328ft high and can lift prefabricated hull and superstructure sub-assemblies weighing up to 1,000 tons each.

Very innovative developments in heavy load lifting and transport techniques for the shipyard and offshore industries are advanced transfer and launch methods, which offer more cost effective ways of building ships and offshore structures. Initially, a hydraulic transfer unit was developed in 1977 from transfer systems employed in civil and heavy engineering, the main advantage being to move large sections of a ship with a greater degree of precision and transfer a completed hull into a launching position. Since then this new aspect of shipyard construction has rapidly developed and two companies that are prominent in the field are the Pearlson Engineering Co Inc, with its 'Syncrolift' shiplift and transfer systems, and Hydranautics, both in the United States.

Nearly 150 Syncrolift systems have been installed in 58 countries throughout the world, the latest being at Todd Pacific Shipyards Corp, Los Angeles division. Completed in 1983 the company say that the Todd Syncrolift is the largest shiplift in the world, 655ft long and 106ft wide, with a lifting capacity for vessels up to 48,000 dwt. An adjacent transfer system will enable the yard to service five maximum size ships ashore at one time.

Hydranautics has designed a hydraulic chain jack elevator and a hydraulic wheeled transfer system (bogie train) which has been installed in the PNOC Marine Corporation's Shipbuilding and Ship Repair

Stiffening bars being placed into position at the Scott Lithgow yard prior to automatic welding. *Scott Lithgow*

complex in the Philippines. The elevator has a maximum lift capacity of 1,200 long tons. Operating in conjunction with the shiplift system at the yard is the 'pitless' wheeled transfer system which has 10 bogie cars. Besides lifting and transferring ships, the system can also be used for ship retrieval and other useful shipyard tasks.

Hydranautics also has a concept to utilise graving docks for production, using hydraulic chain jacks with temporary crane towers to manoeuvre and lower large units into and around the dock without large overhead cranes and flooding. The concept is an adaption of Hydranautics' portable pier and deck lifting system, where entire ship sections weighing 1,000 tons to 4,000 tons could be skidded to the graving dock, lowered to the bottom of the graving dock and then skidded into position for alignment and welding. The method would eliminate the need to flood the graving dock for section movements, and also eliminate the risk of handling unstable ship sections during the flotation period.

Machinery for working ships' plates and sections has become larger and more powerful since World War 2, and this is very much due to the building of mammoth-sized tankers and offshore structures, but there have also been developments in the preparation of shipbuilding steels before fabrication.

Most materials, plates and sections are nowadays shot-blasted to remove rust and mill scale. This is generally executed by the impeller wheel type where the abrasive is thrown against the steel surface at high velocity. Following shot-blasting the material immediately passes through an airless spray painting plant to be automatically sprayed with a priming paint of controlled thickness.

Since World War 2 welding has almost totally displaced riveting in ship construction. Initially, welding was used in ships as a means of repairing various metal parts, then during World War 1 various authorities undertook research into welding. But it was not until World War 2 that all-welded ships came into their own, when the Americans built the Liberty ships.

The welding process used in shipbuilding is of the fusion welding type where welding is achieved at a heat source which is largely intense enough to melt the edges of the material to be joined as it traverses along the joint. This method includes gas welding, arc welding and resistance welding.

Although the trend is toward automatic welding, this still represents a small proportion of total welding processes. Most large shipyards use automatic fillet welding machines and deck welders: some employ welding gantries in the prefabrication shops. Portable self-propelled twin-fillet welders consist of a carriage straddling the stiffener and equipped with two welding heads. Either open-arc or submerged-arc welding processes can be used. As a new development in automated welding, a computer-controlled robot system for automatic welding of hull components was developed by NKK of Japan. This was hitherto considered difficult because of the varying hull configuration. An important welding development which is gaining ground is the electro-slag process, with applications in the welding of very thick plates.

The cutting of ship's plates is mostly done using gas cutting techniques. There are two types of gas cutter: those that work by photo-electric scanning of a

Bending rolls and presses are some of the most important machine tools of the shipbuilding industry. The Bonar Hugh Smith 14m × 2,000-ton shipyard roll press, installed in the Gotevreken shipyard, is typical of the company's massive range of roll presses and combines the functions of a set of rolls and a heavy flanging press.   *Bonar Hugh Smith*

drawing and those controlled by magnetic tape produced by a digital computer. This can be done automatically by use of numerically controlled (NC) machines, which even now are being superseded by computerised numerical control (CNC).

The latest development in plate cutting is the gas-shielded plasma-arc process where materials such as aluminium, stainless steel, nickel-bearing alloys and those containing copper and other metals can also be cut.

Apart from flame burning, plate edges for welding may be performed mechanically. Plate edge mech-

The Bonar Hugh Smith frame bender is one of a range specially designed for the cold bending of 'offset bulb flat' or 'unequal angle' type frames, which are widely used in modern welded construction, where the edge of the web is directly welded to the shell of the ship. The 400-ton bender in the picture is forming a pair of bulb flats. The 700-ton machine was developed to deal with the massive sections involved in the construction of very large carriers and tankers.
Bonar Hugh Smith

anical planing machines have been a common enough tool in shipyards for some considerable time and recently the introduction of a heavy duty edge milling machine has been made possible by improvements in cutting tools.

One of the most important machine tools in a shipyard is the bending rolls. The conventional machine is the pyramid type, so named because the top roller lies above the bottom two rollers in pyramid fashion. The most versatile rolls is the four-roll combined pyramid plate bending and straightening rolls. For shipyards of high output building medium to large vessels, the heavy duty combined bending rolls and flanger is an essential piece of equipment. The vertical plate bender is another machine of modern development, able to roll ultra-thick plates.

A press can execute most of the type of work performed by a set of rolls but is about one-third cheaper. On the other hand a set of rolls is quicker to set up and does not require the same degree of skill to operate. All modern presses should be provided with self-contained electric-hydraulic pumping units and motors. For shipbuilding purposes portal type presses with a ring frame or gap presses, are greatly used. Portal type ring frame presses are very versatile tools and many are designed with an offset ram. A further and recent development to this is to arrange the bottom table and ram to traverse across the portal frame. Gap presses are probably the most useful general purpose machines in shipyards, and the trend is towards machines of relatively high power incorporating the drive mechanism within the main frame, with access from top and rear.

Ships' frames once used to have to be furnaced before bending but now there is powerful machinery available that can bend them cold. There are two types of frame benders; one that is capable of accepting any rolled section and another that excludes channels and bulb angles. All bars are bent in pairs with a 'dummy' bar and templates of some form are required.

Plate guillotines or shears are useful tools in shipyards and should be provided with power-operated clamping. Some guillotines bevel the plate at the same time as shearing. For pipe flanging the latest development is a machine developed by Appledore Shipbuilders/Fogg & Young, which is available with micro-processor control to give fully automated operation.

A world leader in the design and manufacture of machine tools for heavy metal-working in the shipbuilding industry is Bonar Hugh Smith Ltd of Glasgow. The company — a member of the Low & Bonar Group — is probably best known for its massive roll presses, which range in power from 600 to 3,000 tonnes. The 3,000-tonne press is the largest and most powerful standard machine of its type in the world today and is capable of working plates up to 16.5m long by 60mm thick, and combines the functions of a set of rolls and a heavy flanging press. One size down from this — a 14m by 2,000-tonne shipyard roll press — was installed in the Gotevrken shipyard at Arendal in Sweden. The company's ring frame presses range from 300 tonnes up to 2,000 tonnes and are designed for plate forming on a flow line basis. The ram and table have a motorised traverse within the portal opening, thus allowing, along with the 360° rotary adjustment, tools to be positioned accurately and the full width of plate to be worked accurately. Other press type machines by the company include hydraulic press brakes and gap presses.

The advent of very large bulk carriers and tankers posed many problems in that much larger and more powerful machines were needed to deal with the massive construction sections involved. To meet this need Bonar Hugh Smith developed in close association with the British Ship Research Association (BSRA) a numerically-controlled ship's frame bender, the first of its kind. This 700-tonne frame bender is capable of bending frames up to 1.2m deep and has been designed so that it can operate with the Kongsberg numerically-controlled frame-marking system, as are the standard frame benders of the company, which are made in powers of 200, 400 and 600 tons.

The Hydrolevel plate straightening machine is also manufactured by the company, having a rolling speed of 9m per minute, and designed to be incorporated in yards employing flow-line production techniques. Probably the most impressive of Bonar Hugh Smith's plate bending machines is its vertical plate bender. The range of such machines is from 300 to 5,000 tonnes force and for plates up to 4.5m wide and from 20mm to over 200mm thick, rolled cold. The 5,000-tonne plate bender is widely used by manufacturers of offshore rigs and platforms.

Plate edge preparation evolved from the introduction of welded ships, and Bonar Hugh Smith's answer was to develop the Edgemill, a heavy-duty high-performance milling machine capable of machining single and double bevels and Js along the plate edge at a much faster rate than that achieved by planing. Several sizes of Edgemill are available, the largest of which can prepare the edges of plates up to 18m and longer. In addition to mild steel, the machine is particularly useful for preparing the edges of high-tensile plates and has a number of features incorporated in its design.

The Bonar Hugh Smith 1,000ton ring frame press with traversing ram and table.   *Bonar Hugh Smith*

A 5,000-ton vertical plate bender by Bonar Hugh Smith undergoing tests in the maker's works. This type of machine is widely used by manufacturers of offshore rigs and platforms. *Bonar Hugh Smith*

3

Ships' Equipment

Ships' equipment — like ships themselves — has undergone radical changes since World War 2. The need to improve cargo-handling rates, reduce manning, minimise turnabout times and maximise earning capacity, safety and comfort has produced developments in practically every department concerned with a vessel's functions.

Beginning with deck machinery and equipment, the first steel patent hatches were produced just over 30 years ago and since then have developed in size, design, operation and efficiency. Today, virtually all dry cargo ships and bulk carriers are equipped with them in some form. Construction is usually of plated steel, stiffened with webs or stiffeners. Nowadays, box-girder sections are becoming more popular. Modern patent hatch covers can be of several types — single or two-part, or multi-section; side or end shifting, rolling,

folding or lifting. One or two-part covers are used on ships such as bulk carriers and OBO's. Of all the multi-section types the single pull is most common, being first introduced in 1949. This type is where all the hatch covers are opened simultaneously by a single operation. Folding hatch covers have allowed for the possibility of extending hatch area by reducing the hatch cover stowage area.

Considering cargo-handling arrangements, the major factor influencing the port time of a ship is the speed of loading and discharge. Methods of cargo-handling vary according to local conditions and particular trades. Argument still ensues whether shore cranes are preferable to ships' gear. It is true to say that the use of ships without cargo-handling gear is restricted to well-defined routes with good shore facilities. Until about 30 years ago derricks were universally employed for ship-

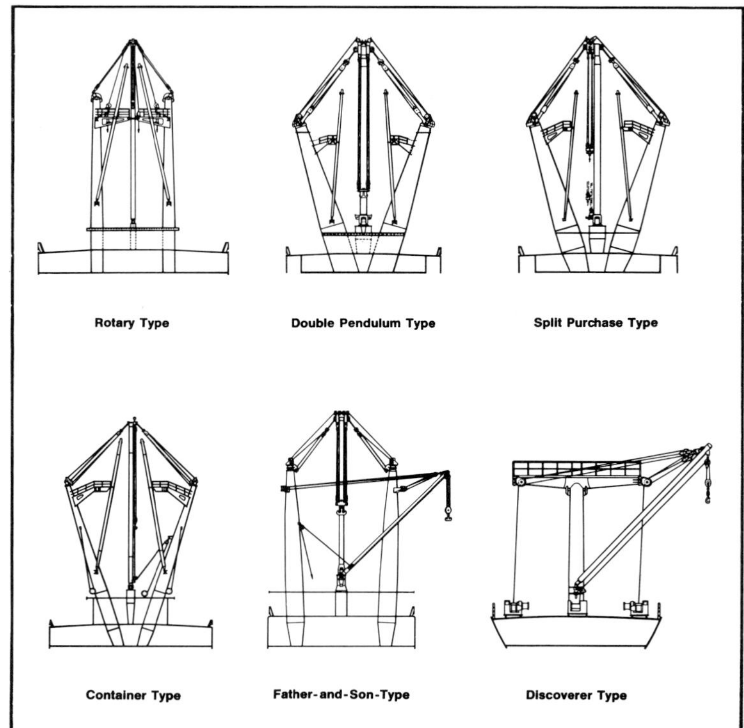

Different types of derrick.
Blohm Voss

board handling, being usually steam or electric-powered. Then studies in the 1950s into the use of cranes concluded that they could considerably improve loading rates. The main reason for this was because of the restricted ability of the union purchase gear, the type most often used then. There has since been extensive developments in the design of electric and hydraulic deck cranes. Nevertheless, there are still certain applications where the derrick is favoured over cranes. Deck cranes can be divided into three broad categories according to their powering; electric, electro-hydraulic and hydraulic. Within each category there are variations according to whether the power is tapped from the ship's main supply or is incorporated in the crane and thus, independent. Fifteen years or so ago the average capacity was three tons, but this has now increased to 10 tons and more. The increased demand for flexibility in cargo-handling has led to the development of twin cranes mounted on a revolving turret between adjacent holds. An alternative to this is the system of 'team' cranes; single cranes loaded in tandem at opposite ends of a hatch. Then in the early 1960s gantry cranes were introduced that ran on tracks outboard of the hatches.

Heavy lifts have been another post-war development. The Norwegian, Christian Smith was among the first to successfully tackle the problem of deep-sea heavy lift transportation and had significant influence on the heavy lift scene between the wars. Immediately after World War 2 Ben Lines became involved in heavy lift shipments and this aspect of a ship's functions rapidly developed.

Among recent developments in cargo handling is a new heavy lift design by Speedcranes Ltd, which incorporates two 100-ton heavy lift cranes arranged with only one mast for support but capable of working over either side of the vessel and serving hatches both fore and aft. They were supplied to two Pacific Steam Navigation Co ships built by Scott Lithgow. Yet another design development is by Babcock-Moxey, which is a continuous unloading system known as the Samsun unloader, for installation on board large bulk carriers. The system, which consists essentially of a gantry straddling the hatches and mounted on rails running the length of the hold, from which is suspended a bucket elevator, would enable such ships to discharge cargo at wharves with few facilities.

Manoeuvring devices have developed greatly since the last world war and include controllable pitch propellers, steerable propellers, cycloidal propellers, tunnel side thrusters and retractable side thrusters, jet thrusters, Y-bow thrusters, active and bow rudders. These devices are of greatest use in approaching dock and berthing, negotiating narrow channels or coming alongside a mooring in an open sea.

Although there are other reasons, improved manoeuvrability can be a prime one for fitting controllable pitch propellers. This is obtained by faster response, matching of main machinery to the propeller, and better hydrodynamic conditions at the propeller. Steerable propellers are essentially mounted on the end of vertical transmission tubes as outboard stern drives, but can also be fitted in wells. The propeller is driven through bevelled gears. Cycloidal propellers use the principle of rotating blades guided on a cycloidal curve.

The Kawasaki KT-B side thruster, latest model by the company. *Kawasaki*

This idea was submitted by an Austrian engineer, J. M. Voith, over 40 years ago and the Voith Schneider propeller is now fitted on many tugs and other small craft requiring high manoeuvrability.

The quest for increased manoeuvrability on all types of ship has led to an extraordinary variety of thruster units. Tunnel side thrusters are commonly referred to as bow thrusters because they are normally (but not essentially) fitted in that position. A tunnel thruster is basically a fixed straight tunnel through the ship fitted with an axial propeller type pump. The pump is mounted on a streamlined nacelle, while the propeller blades may be of fixed or variable pitch. In a pure jet thruster the thrust reaction is obtained by accelerating a fluid through a nozzle across which there is a pressure drop. Thrust is transmitted through a nozzle chamber or piping upstream from the nozzle.

The Schottel Rudderpropeller. *Schottel*

A Schottel SKJ 142 cone jet. *Schottel*

Schottel-Werft is a major manufacturer of manoeuvring and propulsive devices for tugs and other vessels which have special manoeuvring requirements in such areas. The Schottel Propulsion Unit, which incorporates the Schottel Rudderpropeller, has been developed into an all-purpose propulsion system and transfers the engine power into thrust through 360° by use of specially designed gears and a proportional propeller. The range of Schottel Rudderpropellers comes in Z or L-drives and have been fitted on such vessels as the drillship *Glomar Challenger*, the floating crane *Hebe 2*, and the Burness Corlett and Partners (BCP) designed fleet of Type 34 tractor tugs.

Schottel also manufactures the Schottel-Navigator, transverse tunnel thrusters and jet systems, including bow cone and pump jets. The Schottel-Cone-Jet and Pump-Jet have been developed as main drives or as bow manoeuvring aids for extemely shallow draught vessels such as ferries. Schottel's range of devices is from 15 up to 4,500kW, and suitable for all kinds of vessels.

When sail was superseded by steam the stabilising effect of the canvas was lost and designers had to look for other means to stabilise vessels. Over the past 100 years many types of stabilisers have been devised, including bilge keels, moving weights mounted on slides, active and passive tank systems, massive gyros mounted in the body of the ship, and active fin stablisers.

Stabilisation systems have developed considerably in the past 20 years or so, and the various types fall into active or passive categories, the latter involving tanks and a transfer of water, either by natural or forced means. The former will employ some type of fin and mechanical control. Fin stabilisation of ship rolling is now accepted as the norm for many classes of ship such as ferries, passenger and cruise liners and warships. There is also an increasing trend towards stabilisation of cargo vessels, particularly container ships and ro/ro vessels, in order to reduce cargo damage and cargo lashing requirements.

Sperry Marine Systems is a prominent company in the field of navigational aids and also stabilisation systems. In 1955 it introduced the Gyrofin Stabiliser, including an advanced design of aft folding fin, thus improving the water flow abaft the fin box and reducing the space envelope. The company's next development was a control system of sophisticated technology and included the patented Sperry Lift Control that measures lift and compensates for false angles caused by ship movement and disturbed seas, thus avoiding fin cavitation. The total system is one of the most efficient of its kind and since 1965 about 225 sets have been manufactured for a variety of commercial vessels, passenger ships, ferries, container and ro/ro vessels.

The main propulsive machinery of a ship is of two types; reciprocating engines and turbines. Reciprocating engines are mainly internal combustion nowadays; turbines are either steam or gas driven. The major factors affecting the choice of powerplant for a ship are power requirements, weight and space demands, availability of standard units, fuel consumption and costs, and ease of maintenance. There has always been debate regarding the choice between diesel engines and turbines and with increasing oil costs the former has become more efficient and economical in comparison with the latter. Most medium and small diesels are marinised versions of land units and in postwar years more powerful and sophisticated ranges have been developed. Steam turbines have superseded steam engines as the main powerplant for commercial vessels while gas turbines — in many cases combined with some other type of powerplant — have become the automatic choice for military and naval craft. Only a small proportion of merchant ships have gas turbine installations, and some are mentioned in appropriate chapters. The initial and operating costs of gas turbines largely preclude them from being considered for merchant ship propulsion, whereas their easy starting and high performance characteristics make them ideal for military operations.

Japanese shipbuilding companies have become prominent in the field of marine propulsion engines since the war and IHI produce both steam turbines and diesel engines. Under a licence from Sulzer Frères Société Anonyme of Switzerland, IHI manufacturer Sulzer engines including the 32,000bhp IHI/Sulzer 8RND 105 type diesel engine. At its Turbo Machinery works the company produces steam turbines, one being a 50,000shp steam turbine which was installed in the containership *Japan Ambrose*. Kawasaki is another Japanese company involved in marine powerplant manufacturing, and builds diesel engines, and both steam and gas turbines.

Research and development in marine propulsion

units is nowadays very much directed toward economy and versatility in fuel consumption. For example, there have been investigations into the use of heavy fuels for medium speed diesel engines, although this is commonplace for large slow-speed engines as well as the burning of a variety of both solid and liquid fuels in gas turbines. Marine nuclear powerplants are still very much an impractical proposition on a mass commercial basis and much more research and development has to be carried out before they become a viable alternative to present conventional units, although nuclear engines have been installed in some ships and are mentioned in the appropriate chapter.

The most remarkable trend in ships' equipment in this postwar maritime era has been the increasing automation of a vessel's functions, thus reducing the crew complement and its operating costs. The word 'automation' is loosely applied to four areas of marine engineering: navigation, communications, engines and cargo. The advance of marine automation has been in terms of hydraulic and pneumatic rather than electric, and nowadays cargo-handling, engine room operations, navigation and steering and a variety of other tasks are largely controlled by monitoring and control equipment in combination with computer equipment for complex calculations. Machinery control is especially highly developed in modern ships, including those that perform offshore exploration and production tasks.

The navigational field has a variety of automated anti-collision radar equipment which can visually display a large number of targets and show their true and relative courses, then by means of a computer predict collision-avoidance manoeuvres. These systems are called automatic radar plotting aids (ARPA). Since the early 1970s Sperry has been a pioneer in developing collision-avoidance systems and its patented predicted area of danger (PAD) method uses computer-generated graphics to provide a solution to radar plotting problems. A presentation of collision threats is displayed on the planned position indicator (PPI) as graphic hexagonal symbols, the size of which are determined by the operator-selected closest point of approach (CPA) input. The company has also developed the CAS II, a self-contained system that incorporates the PAD approach and is simple to operate and easy and economical to install. Another navigational

A close-up of the Sperry Gyrofin shown in outboard position. The system is designed to provide maximum ordered lift at the specified ship's design speed. The complete unit has a control system which includes a patented lift control that measures fin lift and compensates for false angles. *Sperry*

A 32,000bhp IHI-Sulzer 8RND105 type diesel engine. *IHI*

50,000shp steam turbine built at the Turbo Machinery works of IHI.   *IHI*

Kawasaki's TN3B marine gas turbine.   *Kawasaki*

feature manufactured by Sperry is its SRP-2000 ship control system — an advanced autopilot. Another major company involved in navigational aids as well as marine communications equipment is Marconi, and one of its products is the Marconi Marine Radiolocator 16 radar, complete with true motion unit.

Modern marine communications and radio equipment has become much more powerful, compact and sophisticated compared to the massive hardware of 40 years ago. It is also used as a navigational aid using radio direction finders (RDFs) for pinpointing a ship's position. Receivers are designed to receive signals from a chain of navigation stations and interpret them to give a position fix. Four such systems are DECCA navigator, LORAN, OMEGA and satellite navigators.

One area of automation that has particular significance in the offshore field is dynamic positioning and in recent years the need for dynamic positioning

A revolutionary aspect of ships' equipment in postwar years has been the increasing automation of a ship's functions. Machinery control is especially highly developed in modern shops, including offshore vessels and drilling rigs such as the *Ocean Ben Lancer*.

(DP) systems has been increased by the problems associated with oil drilling and production, particularly in the North Sea. Such problems arise because of the need to be on station for drilling, maintain the position of a support vessel accurately in relation to a fixed structure, for lifting manoeuvres or for inspection work by divers. All these requirements dictate the use of a dynamic positioning system which, in this context, is holding a vessel on-station without using anchors. GEC

Sperry's CA5 II Automatic Radar Plotting Aid installed on a Sealink ferry. *Sperry*

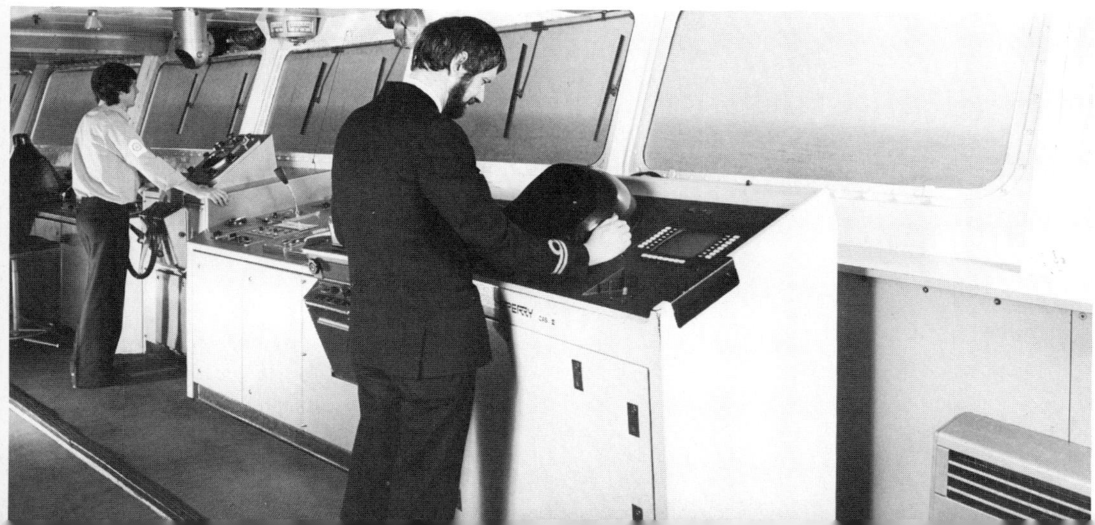

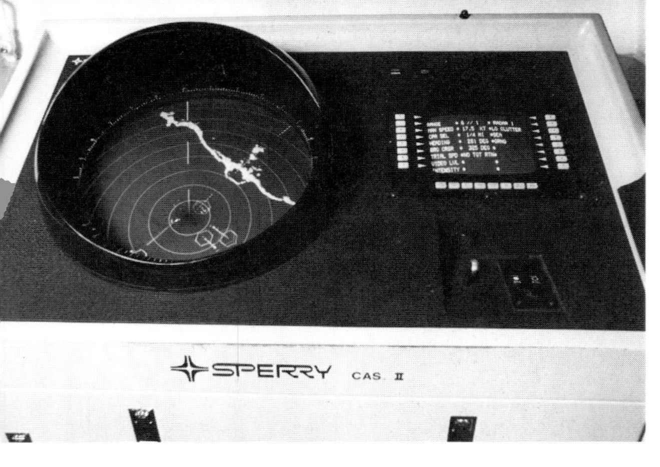

Close-up of Sperry's CAS II display unit. The hexagonal symbols displayed on the PPI represent collision threats. *Sperry*

Electrical Projects have an in-house dynamic positioning system called MAPS which was designed and manufactured by Marconi Space and Defence Systems. It features a central control that is capable of interfacing with any position measurement system — acoustic, taut wire, radio fix, etc.

Automation for bridge controls has defined programmes that will control speed and acceleration. Servomechanisms will convert motor input angles to hydraulic pressures for ahead and astern movements, while there will also be testing and simulation facilities in the system. Monitoring systems will locate and display powerplant faults and the overall effect is to reduce manual operations to an absolute minimum. Complex cargo or ballast pumping systems require

A Marconi Radiolocator 16 radar, complete with truemotion unit, installed on the bridge of a British-registered container ship. *Marconi*

precise remote control, especially considering the large number of valves involved. For instance, a product carrier will have anything from 50 to 250 valves and these will be remotely controlled by means of hydraulic or electro-hydraulic systems.

One trend in control systems is toward the application of microprocessors to replace mini-computers or to undertake roles which are uneconomic with mini-computers. In the long term many of the more straight-forward process control applications will be undertaken by microprocessors. GEC Electric Project's Uni-Control GEM 80 Joystick Control System is microprocessor-based and has an autopilot facility included and is readily extended — in built-up packages — to DP-taut wire based, anchor-assist system, track follow using radio reference, and subsea tracking using acoustic reference.

The final aspect of ships' equipment is not so much concerned with hunks of machinery or computerised black boxes but with the preparation and maintenance of a ship's hull. This factor has become of increasing importance in postwar years because of tight operating costs and port charges. The smoothness of a ship's hull is intrinsically connected with hydrodynamic efficiency and the two factors affecting speed loss are hull roughness and fouling. Consequently, there has always been efforts to reduce fouling and protect the hull against corrosion by means of paints that offer smooth hull surfaces and provide long term protection from fouling and corrosion. Epoxy resins have become recognised as coatings that offer durability, smooth finish, etc, but tend to be more expensive than ordinary paints and require more skill in application. Plastic coatings and vinyls are also in the forefront as efficient, yet reasonably priced means of coating a hull. A variety of hull scrubbing machines has also been developed to keep the underwater hull clean in between the ship's regular drydocking for inspection and maintenance.

There is every reason to suppose that there will be even more effort and development directed toward this aspect of ships' equipment.

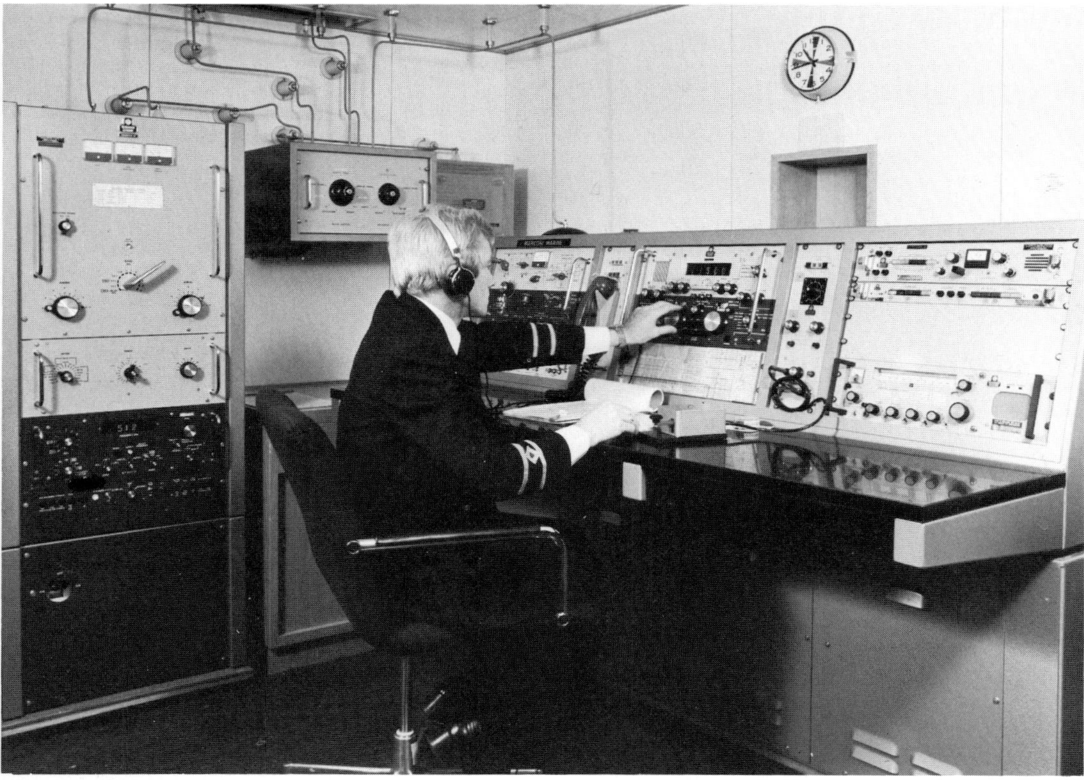

Modern marine radio equipment is much more powerful, compact and sophisticated compared to the massive hardware of 40 years ago. Compare the Marconi wireless installation photographed aboard the RMS *Orion* in 1947 (*top*) with the two Marconi Yeoman receivers, Worldspan transmitter and amplifier, Lodestone direction-finder and Marconi broadcast receiver on a modern container ship (*above*) *Marconi*

4
Oil Tankers

The oil tanker — which is a specialised carrier of oil in bulk — is one of the largest and most important vessels in the world's shipping fleets. It is distinguished from the general cargo carrier and other types by its long low hull. The carriage of oil in bulk demands special precautions and a common practice in tanker design is to site all machinery, accommodation and navigation spaces right aft. A catwalk or walkway is provided to give safe access fore and aft during heavy weather, the low deck being frequently awash during such times. A tanker's block coefficient (ratio of its underwater volume to a circumscribing block) is usually about 0.8 and economic speed is 16-20kts.

The hull is divided into a number of tanks by means of oiltight longitudinal and transverse bulkheads. There are two longitudinal bulkheads for ships up to 35m beam (Lloyd's Rules), and three for greater beam. The framing is longitudinal, with transverse web frames located at intervals within the tanks to provide transverse strength. In two or more positions are double bulkheads providing narrow spaces called cofferdams; these are for strength and to lessen the hazards of fire spreading from the forecastle or engine room to the tanks. Each tank is connected by pipeline to the pump room. Structural strength considerations are of prime importance in tankers and in order to reduce the still water bending moment (SWBM), and thus make lighter scantlings possible, the large tankers have certain tanks near amidships arranged as permanent empty spaces. Tankers which carry lubricating or crude oil are fitted with internal heating systems to keep the cargo at the right temperature and enable it to be pumped out.

As an explosive mixture is formed when oil vapour comes into contact with air, it is essential to ensure that any foul gas accumulation can readily escape. One time at which the gas concentration will be within the explosive region is during discharge, and it is then essential that one or both of the gas concentrations are outside the explosive limit. This is achieved by use of inert gas systems which ensure that oil or ballast pumped from a tank are not replaced by air but by a gas concentration which has an oxygen concentration below the danger limit.

Before considering the history and development of oil tankers since 1945 it would be well to present a short synopsis on how their valuable cargo came to be the ubiquitous fuel of modern civilisation. Since earliest times, pitch or bitumin (crude oil weathered by wind or sun) has been used to seal ships' seams and the joints of buildings. Oil was used centuries ago by the peoples of Burma, while early Iranian lamps were lit by this black gold.

Baku, on the shores of the Caspian Sea, is one of the world's earliest oil areas, the natural gas that escaped to the surface from this region, and accidently lit in some remote age, became known as the famous 'eternal fires'. By the 18th century the oil trade in this part of the world was flourishing, but oil as a big business started in the latter half of the 19th century in the new world of the Americas — especially when the lights of American oil lamps — lit by the oil from sperm whales — began to flicker because of the decimation of the whale herds.

Other sources were sought and 'rock oil', located below the earth's surface in western Pennsylvania, was found to be usable. It was there that the first oil boom started in the 1860s, and gushers shot up around the

An early tanker, the *Wiiri* of 1921. *Real Photos*

The *World Liberty* was built in the early postwar years, and commissioned in 1949. *Real Photos*

town of Pithole in that State, which became the wildest of all boom towns.

Then a new 'land of grease' was discovered in northern Ohio and eastern Indiana — the Lima Field. In 1901 a low circular mound known as 'Big Hill', just outside Beaumont, Texas — and later to be charmingly known as Spindletop — rose to oil fame when a 1,200ft hole that had been drilled suddenly exploded to become the largest gusher the American continent had ever seen up to that time. In 1906 large oil reserves were found in Tulsa, along with other finds at the time and later, and the oil began to flow to international markets — including China.

In Europe, Baku began to be exploited in the late 19th century, then in 1908 the first of the great Iranian oilfields in the Middle East was tapped. This part of the world was to later prove to hold the largest reserves of oil riches. More than half the world's reserves were under its sandy grounds, and since 1945 the oil has flowed in increasing abundance. It then began to dawn on scientists, economists and politicians that no matter how vast were the world's oil reserves, the insatiable thirst of modern civilisation was rapidly depleting them. Estimates predicted that this form of fossil energy would run dry either within decades or a hundred years or so, depending on the pessimism or optimism of the pundit. What was agreed, however, was that a limit existed. It remains to be seen whether the oil tanker becomes a metal dinosaur of the seas or is usefully employed in other fuel-carrying capacities. In the meantime it has grown to be the largest of all merchant vessels.

As regards the ships themselves, in the early days of the industry oil was conveyed by sea in barrels stowed in the holds of sailing ships, just as wine, molasses or any other liquid was carried. Then in 1886 a remarkable little steamship, the *Gluckhauf*, was launched on Tyneside. This 2,307-ton vessel had three sets of sails but bore a striking resemblance to the tankers of today, and can be considered the world's first real oil tanker and the father of the modern tanker. During the next 30 years, as the oil trade expanded, it was general practice to convert ordinary cargo steamers into oil carriers, but because their engines were invariably amidships, this practice was both wasteful and dangerous. There were also new buildings, and in the 1890s 18 to 20 tankers a year were being constructed, having no double bottoms in the cargo tank section and with oil being carried right out to the ship's side. The year 1892 saw the advent of the first tanker to be allowed to pass through the Suez Canal with a cargo of oil. She was the *Murex* and her historical voyage through the canal was made on 24 August. Previous to this tankships had been forbidden to pass through the canal, which had been opened in 1869.

A major step in tanker design came in 1906 when a Lloyd's Register surveyor, Joseph Isherwood, resigned from the Classification Society to develop what came to be known as the 'Isherwood System', a system of longitudinal framing. Then in the 1920s the large scale building of purpose-designed tankers began. In 1920 Cammel Laird and Co built an all-welded cargo ship, the *Fullagar*, and by 1927 there were several all-welded barges and all-welded tankers started to appear in 1934. During World War 2 the most successful standard tanker — the T2 — was designed. Between

A tanker moored alongside Amoco's jetty to deliver crude oil to the company's Milford Haven refinery. *Amoco*

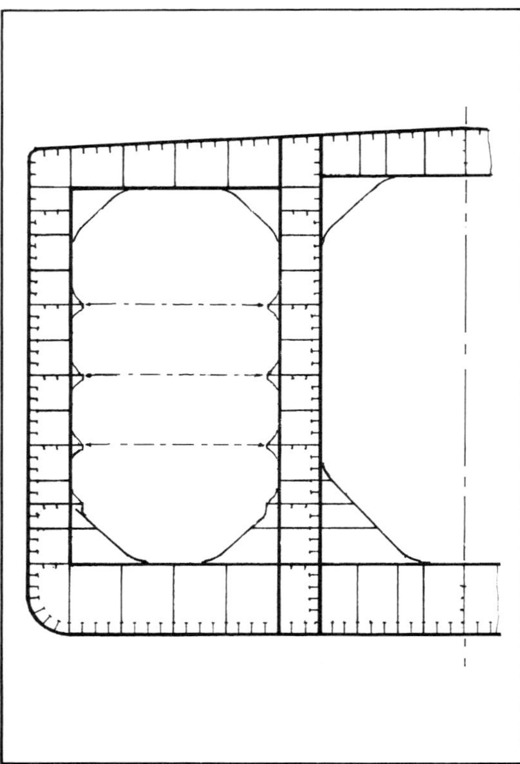

Typical mid-section of a first generation 500,000 dwt tanker.

The Shell tanker *Gari*, a 75,000cu m capacity vessel owned and managed by Shell Tankers (UK) Ltd under the British flag. *Shell*

1942 and 1945 a total of 481 T2-SE A1 tankers were constructed.

The end of the war saw some fundamental changes in the oil industry. Attention was focused on the Middle East fields as a source of supply to Western Europe, while the USA, due to its vastly increased internal consumption, was rapidly becoming an importer rather than an exporter of oil. To overcome the problem of long distance between the Middle East wells and consumers several pipelines were laid to parts in the East Mediterranean, as instanced by the trans-Arabian pipeline which was completed in December 1950.

As the oil industry grew after the war so did the size of tankers. But there was a limit to this vessel growth — or so it seemed — governed mainly by two factors. The first of these was that up to 1950 most Middle East crude (which forms the greatest proportion of the world's market) was refined near the source of production; for the most part it was — and still is — uneconomical to carry large quantities of a single refined product. The second limiting factor was that the maximum size of a vessel was limited by the Suez Canal requirements. This canal is the shortest and most convenient route from the Middle East to the oil consuming parts of Western Europe. These two factors meant that vessels were restricted to around 25,000 to 50,000 tons.

In 1951 Shell-Royal Dutch fitted an experimental gas turbine in the tanker *Auris* (8,221grt), and also carried out an immense tanker building programme. The *Velletia*, completed in 1950, was the largest tanker yet built in Britain. Tanker construction in the UK and the Continent at this stage reached new heights, with the trend toward faster and larger vessels to meet the requirements of longer voyages and increased production. Germany, Italy and Japan began to build their tanker fleets while three independent tanker fleets — the Ludwig, Niarchos and Onassis groups of companies

The IHI-built *Globtik Tokyo*, of 477,000 dwt, was the world's largest tanker in 1973. *IHI*

— appeared on the scene. But the seven major oil companies also had their own fleets. These 'seven sisters', as they are commonly referred to, are the Standard Oil Co of New Jersey (known as EXXON in America but ESSO to the rest of the world), Standard Oil of New York (SOCONY, which eventually became Mobil), Standard Oil of California (SOCAL), Gulf, Texaco Royal Dutch Shell (SHELL) and British Petroleum (BP). At around this time welding was also being universally employed in tanker construction.

So it was that the economics of oil transportation dictated that tankers should become increasingly larger. The 23,000-ton tanker appeared in 1944 and the 300,000-ton ship in 1968. The terms applied to such giant tankers give some idea of this growth in a short space of 24 years. The first term was 'super', which was later followed by 'monster', then even later by 'mammoth'. This is now replaced by 'behemoth'. The *British Realm* — built by Fairfields, Goven, in 1952 — became at that time the world's largest tanker at 28,000 dwt, but the following years saw a steady increase in size. From 1956 to 1973 the title 'world's largest tanker' had been claimed by nine different ships, one holding the honour for a mere seven days. The following list of world record holders illustrates the rapid growth of tanker size during that period — all were built in Japan:

Name	Dwt	Launched
Sinclair Petrolore	56,089	1956
Universal Leader	85,515	1957
Universal Apollo	104,520	1959
Nissho Maru	130,250	1962
Tokyo Maru	157,290	1966
Idemitsu Maru	206,000	1966
Universe Ireland	326,000	1968
Nisseki Maru	372,700	1971
Globtik Tokyo	477,000	1973

The first vessel to reach 100,000 tons dwt was the *Universe Apollo*. In 1962 another 100,000-ton tanker, the *Manhattan*, was delivered, built to the order of the Niarchos organisation. With a deadweight tonnage of 108,590, the *Manhattan* had a number of design innovations. For instance, instead of the normal deep girders on the centreline she had a continuous centreline wash bulkhead. Heavy doubler plates were fitted at both deck and bottom shell, while another unusual feature for a large tanker was the twin screws.

SS *Manhattan* — when built the largest tanker in the world — before modification. She had an icebreaking bow attached to make an historic voyage through the North-West Passage.

The *Manhattan* was used in a full-scale experiment in transporting oil from Alaska via the North-West Passage to the Eastern USA. Fitted with an icebreaking bow and a 9ft wide wedge-shaped ice-belt along the waterline (one of many other changes), the ship eventually arrived in Halifax, Nova Scotia on 28 August 1969. She then proceeded to Thule in Greenland and, assisted by Canadian and US icebreakers, forced her way through the ice, eventually arriving at Prudhoe Bay on 19 September 1969. Soon after, she commenced her return journey and arrived back off the East Coast on 12 November 1969.

The Six-Day War of 1967 provided the impetus for a new generation of tankers. The consequent closure of the Suez Canal because of the war meant that tankers had to be re-routed round the Cape of Good Hope: a much longer route that reduced the number of journeys per year as well as increasing the time per journey. The cost of transporting the crude rose rapidly and dramatically, and as the capital cost per ton tends to be far less for larger vessels, this obviously set designers thinking in the direction of designing mammoth tankers.

SS *Lampas* is an example of the VLCC; a Shell vessel of 314,000 dwt, she was built by Harland and Wolf in 1976. *Shell*

Up to then they had no experience of overcoming the engineering problems presented by fabricating vessels over 300m long, able to withstand the severe stresses caused by heavy seas. In the event they succeeded only too well and now giant tankers of 500,000 dwt or so plough the oceans. The initials VLCC (very large crude carrier) and ULCC (ultra large crude carrier) have been given to such floating giants, the former being in the 200,000-300,000 dwt class and the latter being of 400,000 dwt or more.

Two prime examples of gargantuan tankers are the twins *Batillus* and *Bellamya*, built by Chantier de L'Atlantique of St Nazairex in 1976. The *Batillus* had a deadweight of 533,662 tons and is managed by Societe Maritime Shell under the French flag. Her principal dimensions are: overall length 414m (1,358ft), breadth 63m (206.8ft), draught 28.6m (93.8ft). The main propulsion machinery comprises two Atlantique Stal Laval AP 32/85 steam turbine sets, each developing 23,830kW (32,400shp) at 86rpm. Superheated steam is generated by two Atlantique Foster Wheeler ESD3 boilers, each capable of delivering 125ton/hr of steam at 73kg/sq cm and 515°C. The present world's largest is the *Seawise Giant*, converted at NKK's Tsu Shipyard in Japan in 1981. This 560,000 dwt tanker has an overall length of 458.45m, a moulded breadth of 68.8m and a moulded draught of 24,563m.

At one time many people doubted whether the Suez Canal would ever be reopened, but when with international co-operation Egypt went ahead and cleared the canal in 1975, along with a huge expansion contract aimed at increasing its capacity, the venture proved justifiable. More than 1,200 vessels used the canal in its first year of operation since the reopening, including 11 VLCCs, the largest being the 231,759 dwt *Norse King*, making the special transit with tugs. The expansion programme in its final completion would allow for 260,000 dwt vessels and above. So the canal, whose closure stimulated the growth of oil tankers, profited in the end. Nevertheless, it is difficult to forecast how large such tankers will become. One disadvantage is that mammoth-sized vessels require special berthing facilities and large dry docks for maintenance and repair, while being only able to operate from ports capable of accommodating their deep draughts.

The largest proportion of tankers now being constructed seems to fall in the 205,000-285,000 dwt band, accounting for almost half the total world tanker tonnage. Interestingly enough, 80,000 dwt 'ecology class' tankers underwent a boom in 1979, showing that this is the size of ships deemed suitable for profitable operations in the 1980s. These 80,000-tonners have their length and draught reduced and beam increased, compared to older tankers of this size, thus allowing access to restricted draught ports on the US Gulf and East Coast. Also, due to insistence by the

Until recently the world's largest oil tanker, the SS *Batillus* entered service with Societe Maritime Shell in June 1976 and weighs in at 553,662 dwt. *Shell*

Amoco's oil production platform in the UK sector of the North Sea; it employs two SPBMs and was the first of the British oil strikes in the North Sea. *Amoco*

US that all tankers trading to its ports should conform to the Inter-Governmental Maritime Organisation (IMO) Tanker Safety and Pollution Prevention (TSPP) regulations, it has been necessary to include segregated ballast tanks, crude oil washing, inert gas systems and improved radar and navigation equipment. Another feature of these tankers is the use of slow speed marine diesels, which are claimed to reduce fuel consumption by as much as 40%, compared to older tankers of the same deadweight.

The Shell tanker *Drupa* loading crude oil from SPAR which transferred the first oil from Shell/Esso's Brent oilfield in the North Sea. *Shell*

The 79,999 dwt limit of the new tankers arises from the Average Freight Assessment (AFRA) Large Range I category, which is the upper limit of the 45,000-80,000 dwt range used by the London Tanker Broker Panel for the freight rate evaluation. For this reason the tankers are known as AFRAMAX tankers. The vessels can pass through the Suez Canal well laden, and are also of suitable size for Japan's short-haul routes.

One interesting aspect of oil production and transportation is the offshore fields. As North Sea exploration and exploitation moved into ever deeper waters and further away from land, so pipelaying became more technically difficult and prohibitive in cost: the size and lifetime of a reservoir had to warrant such an expensive exercise. A much cheaper and easier answer was offshore loading. The first systems were located in sheltered waters near the coast, or in estuaries. The conventional buoy mooring system (CBM) has a tanker moored to a number of buoys, each attached to an anchor. But this system is sensitive to inclement weather, which means a downtime in loading operations when rough weather occurs. To overcome this disadvantage designs developed toward single-point buoy mooring systems (SPBMs), where the tanker is moored by bow hawsers to a single rotatable mooring point and allowed to swing, thus minimising mooring forces.

The SPBM is a relatively inexpensive method of mooring and loading oil tankers in offshore areas and at present there are over 120 units installed worldwide, principally in offshore Mexico, Louisiana, Indonesia and the North Sea. In the North Sea the Montrose Field — the first of the British oil strikes in that area — employs two SPBMs: the Beryl Field also has one. The Thistle Field was planned to have a single anchor-leg mooring system (SALM), as also the Fulmar Field. Another design is the exposed location single-point mooring system (ELSBM) as installed in the Auk Field, while a further development is the SPAR buoy mooring system (SBM) which is an extremely large unit incorporating storage tanks and — unlike the others — is manned. The Brent Field in the North Sea has a SPAR system installed.

A general view of the ELSBM during securing of the anchor chains when installed on the Auk oilfield in the North Sea. *Shell*

The 75,000cu m tanker SS *Gadila* owned and managed by Shell Tankers (UK) Ltd.   *Shell*

The 84,688 dwt *Esso Warwickshire*, which is the fourth in a series of six 'County' class supertankers. Launched in 1962, the vessel was designed for the economic transport of the crude oil, principally from Mediterranean ports to the Esso refineries at Milford Haven and Fawley.   *Esso*

Considering the construction of very large tankers, one technique that has been developed is the building of the hull in two parts. One company that has adopted this two-part building technique is Scott Lithgow, which built facilities to cater for this type of construction. The block system of construction — as with other ships — has also been extensively used in tanker construction.

To give an idea of tanker economics, an American paper written in 1973 anaylsed the costs of large versus small tankers. This study revealed that it cost at that time $150million to build a fleet of ten 50,000 dwt tankers as against $78million for a 500,000 dwt tanker. Present day costs would naturally far exceed these figures but the cost difference would probably be the same.

The construction cost per deadweight ton decreases with increase in tanker size, while the manning requirement for a 500,000 dwt is nearly the same as for a much smaller one. The capital cost of automation equipment forms a smaller percentage of the total cost of a larger ship, therefore a high degree of automation becomes more attractive as consumption costs increase.

The hull maintenance and repair costs per deadweight ton for large vessels, compared to smaller ones, have been found to be considerably reduced; the same applies for machinery. Fuel costs were found to represent nearly 35% of the total operating costs of a large tanker at that time. With the massive price rises that have occurred since then, this figure would probably top 50%. In fact, there has been a tendency to convert some turbine-powered tankers to diesel. As size increases so fuel consumption per deadweight ton decreases, assuming a constant speed. Administrative costs are minimal and need not be considered.

Although the above factors point favourably to large tankers and their construction, the very dimensions of these ships restrict their operation to given trade routes. Before an oil company can commit itself to large

The 155,612 dwt Ben Line *Grey Warrior*. *Ben Lines*

The IHI-built *World Texas* 52,080 dwt. *IHI*

tankers it must have an ample supply of crude oil at a suitable loading point. This crude oil must be located at ports with suitable handling facilities.

Tankers in our modern day world have brought home the drastic effects of pollution. It is estimated that about half a million tons of oil pollute the oceans each year. The most significant type of casualty that causes pollution seems to be structural failure, while groundings and collisions are other major causes. A series of tanker casualties around the US coast in the three months of 1966-67 brought about international measures to reduce pollution, and such measures have been incorporated in the AFRAMAX tankers mentioned earlier.

It would appear that the VLCCs and ULCCs — contrary to popular belief — can transport a given quantity of oil over a given distance safer than their smaller counterparts. Probably the most widely quoted statistic on these giant vessels is full-throttle-reverse stopping distances from cruising speed. For 16kts this manoeuvre requires four nautical miles, whereas a T-2 tanker requires something less than a nautical mile. However, these mammoth vessels approach congested waters at most at about 6kts, and stopping distances are significantly reduced to something like three-quarters of a nautical mile.

Finally, there are coastal tankers, which are smaller versions of the ocean-going tanker. The coastal tanker was virtually unknown in Britain before World War 1, then the development of motor driven coastal tankers made great strides in the 1930s. The trips of a coastal tanker are unusually short, and it may be employed on the same route between ports only a few sailing hours apart. Such vessels generally have a navigating bridge on the poop while the tank top, constructed in the clear space between the poop and forecastle, is on two levels. The centre section is a few feet higher, forming what is known as the trunk deck.

The coastal tanker formed an integral part of the American petroleum distribution system up to the late 1950s until the tug/barge system challenged its dominance and almost brought about its near demise. Recently, there has been a revival of interest in this ship type as a viable proposition, as exemplified by the *MV Northern Sun*, which, after many studies, was built for a specific mission by its owners, Sun Transport, and commenced operations in 1981.

Another coastal tanker of recent construction is the *Esso Plymouth*, built by Cochrane Shipbuilders in 1980. It is the first British-built ship of any substantial size to feature a resiliently mounted superstructure, and includes a Schilling rudder and a heavy fuel Allen diesel engine. The *Esso Plymouth* replaces a time-chartered vessel operating mainly out of Fawley Refinery, carrying gasoline, kerosene, aviation fuel, diesel and other light products.

The coastal tanker *Esso Plymouth*, equipped with bow thruster and Schilling rudder, shows her exceptional manoeuvrability during sea trials. *Esso*

5
Chemical and Liquid Gas Carriers

Three types of specialised tanker have evolved since World War 2: chemical, liquid petroleum gas (LPG) and liquid natural gas (LNG) vessels. Each will be dealt with separately in this chapter.

Chemical carriers

A growth has taken place in the chemical and related industries in the past 20 years or so, and this is reflected in the increased demand for marine bulk transport and facilities which incorporate means of maintaining the quality of the product and ensuring safe containment. From this demand has evolved chemical tankers of increasing sophistication which are related through a family of solvents and multi-products tankers to earlier generations of parcel tankers.

Today, specialised ships are essentially improvements of the latter — improved for the purpose of transporting in bulk many of the chemical substances produced and consumed by modern industry.

Initially, existing ships were converted as a principal means of satisfying the resultant increase in demand, but during the 1960s purpose-built carriers became more common. Prominent in the trade today are highly sophisticated ships able to carry a very wide range of incompatible and hazardous substances. Such chemical tankers must always be protected from contamination and strict quality control is necessary. Despite the hazardous nature of the substances carried the safety record of bulk chemical tankers is very good.

The substances commonly carried by bulk chemical carriers are petro-chemical products, coal tar products, carbohydrate derivatives, animal vegetable oils and heavy chemicals. Carbon natural products exist naturally in abundance and the traditional bulk liquid 'product' cargoes are paraffins obtained from crude oil by fractional distillation. The aromatic compounds benzene, toluene and xylene, from which are derived some very important commodities, can be obtained as coal tar products. Esters occur in nature in the form of vegetable and animal oils and fats; their composition is

The liquid gas carrier *Bergia* of 1967. *Real Photos*

The chemical tanker *Alchimist Flensburg* (1971).   *Real Photos*

quite different from that of petroleum (mineral) oils, which are almost completely composed of hydrocarbons. The animal and vegetable oils which are used in the manufacture of such widely varying commodities as soap detergents, margarine, etc, have been carried in ships for many years, the main problems being those of maintaining cargo quality. Heavy chemicals are those which are produced in very large quantities and utilised by virtually every manufacturing industry. These include such commodities as sulphuric acid, caustic soda, sulphur, nitric acid, phosphoric acid, etc.

The first tanker designed to carry chemicals in bulk was the *Marine Dow-Chem*, a twin-screw turbine driven vessel built in 1954 for the Marine Chemical Transport Company Inc. Since then designs have become more complex and safety conscious. Chemical tanker design and construction is virtually inseparable from regulatory considerations, the primary influence being the IMO Code which applies to bulk chemicals having significant hazards other than flammability. Three ship types (I, II and III) are provided for in the Code, the most significant difference between the types being their ability to survive specified extents of damage and prevent or limit resultant release of energy. Liquid or vapour standards supplement these criteria.

The chemical tanker type and containment requirements depend on the hazards associated with chemical release, which cover the health and water pollution aspects, reactivity in water and conditions for combustion and explosion. Briefly, Type 1 ships can carry substances whose release would have effects not con-

The *Echoman*, first of two tankers for Rowbotham Tankships Ltd, is a chemical tanker built to carry IMO Type 3 cargoes and also suitable for carrying heavy liquid cargoes with a specific gravity of 1.6. Built by Appledore Shipbuilders Ltd, it entered service in 1982.   *Appledore Shipbuilders Ltd*

Model of the Moss Rosenberg gas/chemical carrier *Igloo Finn* which was delivered in 1981. An identical ship was delivered in 1982. *Moss Rosenberg*

fined to the immediate proximity of vessel and which would therefore constitute a major environmental hazard. Type II ships may carry substances that constitute a more confined hazard, while Type III ships are intended for least hazardous substances. For a Type I ship escape of cargo cannot be tolerated, while for Type II limited release is permissible but significant preventative measures are required. Cargoes for Type III require a more moderate degree of containment.

The design and construction of chemical tankers involves more complicated considerations than those for crude oil tankers. For instance, when considering ship floatability and damage stability, a primary requirement of the IMO Code is that this type of vessel should remain stable and afloat after damage. Damage stability problems encountered can sometimes be resolved by the manner of longitudinal sub-division of the double bottom and arranging the centreline girder to be perforated so that simultaneous port and starboard flooding occurs, providing that resultant free surface effects on stability is acceptable.

For a conventional oil tanker the main concern with hazardous zones is the fire/explosion hazard. This is minimised by excluding sources of ignition from areas where vapour may be present, and introducing inert gas systems. In addition to this, chemical tankers have to take into account toxic dangers. The resultant hull arrangements, in terms of hazardous zones, can be very complex. The hazards of fire on board a chemical tanker necessitate that primary emphasis be placed on prevention as distinct from firefighting capability.

The principal features which affect chemical tanker design scantlings (over and above those applicable to any oil tanker) are specific gravity of cargo and pressure/vacuum valve settings, corrosive characteristics of cargo and quality of materials of construction, tank size and stiffening arrangements, cargo heating arrangements and temperature.

The influence of specific gravity increases the pressures on tank boundaries and may also increase the concentration of loading in the cargo tank area. In addition to minimising release of hazardous vapours, the pressure/vacuum valves control the conditions for replacement of cargo vapour by air and thus minimises the loss by evaporation of highly volatile cargoes. Cargoes which are highly corrosive to mild steel will generally require the use of special materials for tank construction and systems. The austenitic stainless steels have the widest range of compatability with chemicals, possessing good workability characteristics and exhibiting relatively good weldability. The influence of cargo tank size on scantlings is significant only in the absence of internal stiffening, which would otherwise dampen the motion of the liquid within a slack tank and prevent excessive dynamic loading of tank boundaries. Where cargoes are to be carried at high temperature, the resultant thermal stresses may make it necessary to limit the hull bending moment so that an acceptable total stress is not exceeded.

Two chemical tankers of recent construction are the

The products carrier *Esso Bayonne*, 29,121 dwt, built by IHI for Esso Tankers Inc.   *IHI*

Johnson Chemstar and *Johnson Chemsun*, built by Kockums and delivered to their owners, Rederi AB Nordstjernan in 1981. These 38,000 dwt vessels, designed to carry Type II and Type III chemicals, were the largest of their type at the time but are now exceeded by the chemical tanker *Hitra* at 38,229 dwt. Another new building is the gas/chemical carrier *Igloo Finn*, built by Moss Rosenberg and delivered in 1981. An identical sister ship was delivered in 1982.

One offshoot of chemical tankers is the development of parcel chemical carriers, which came from the experience gained in the early 1960s. This experience provided the shipowner with the knowledge to see that he could improve voyage results significantly by utilising the counter movements of many widely differing bulk speciality liquids. Parcel chemical carriers are a type of tank ship purpose-built to carry a variety of bulk liquids requiring specialised cargo-handling and cargo containments. These ships are designed and built to provide exceptional flexibility of cargo tank use and stowage over a wide range of liquid cargo.

The sophisticated modern day parcel carrier should not be confused with the less developed product carrier, or even the chemical carrier, these latter vessels not having the same flexibility. Parcel trade is worldwide, with certain key geographical areas serving as focal points. As such, the design of parcel carriers requires the identification of transportation requirements and associated constraints, the definition of design parameters and variables, the development of a design concept to allow for the identification of ship's characteristics and related costs, and lastly to optimise the technical and commercial aspects.

Finally, there is the product carrier, and whereas chemical tankers are specifically built for the transportation of concentrated sulphuric acid, phosphoric acid, ethylene and other chemicals, product carriers may also carry intermediate oil products. The coating of the tanks determines the quality of a product carrier and a chemical carrier and one company which has particular expertise in this area is IHI. With the increased production and shipping of intermediate oil products from oil-producing countries, IHI has built such product carriers as the 47,803 dwt *Peter Maersk*, completed in 1981, and the 29,121 dwt *Esso Bayonne*, as well as chemical carriers such as the ethylene carrier *Ethylene Unakami* at 45,648 dwt.

LPG carriers

Petroleum gases such as propane and butane, carried in pressure tanks at ambient temperature, have been transported for many years in ships. Then attention was given to their low temperature carriage at ambient pressure. The LPG ship has evolved in the past 25 years or so, designed for the carriage of fuel and fertilisers. More recently still, the LNG ship has been developed for the transport of liquid natural gas as an industrial and domestic fuel.

Prior to 1959 LPG was carried in tanks in fully pressurised conditions, then the introduction of refrigeration plants led to semi-pressurised ships and semi-refrigerated ships. The tanks of early semi-pressurised ships were constructed of carbon steel, with temperatures down to −10°C. Nowadays, −45°C is quite common, where tanks are of cylindrical and horizontal construction. Rapid development has occurred in fully refrigerated ships since the introduction of the first such vessel in 1961. The tanks are prismatic and self-supporting, and designed for a minimum temperature of about −50°C.

Among LPG carriers of recent construction is IHI's

LPG carrier *Genkai Maru*, completed in 1980. This 49,997 dwt vessel has a tank capacity of 80,311cu cm. An LPG/ammonia carrier also built by IHI is the 13,483 dwt *M. P. Grace*. The company also built the LPG carrier *Pioneer Louise* in 1976, this vessel being the first to use Shell's internal insulation system under licence. The system departs from conventional methods in that it involves the basically simple process of spraying polyurethane foam directly on to the flush inner hull plating of a tanker, thus serving both to contain and insulate the cargo of liquid gas.

LNG carriers

The marketing of natural gas was made possible by a new and revolutionary means of shipping gas by sea, which hinged on liquefying the gas by refrigeration to a level of −258°C, at which point the liquid occupies less than 1/600 of its gaseous volume. This means the LNG has to be isolated in insulated and separate containers from the tanker's hull structure, otherwise the steel will be subject to brittle fracture.

Natural gas is composed primarily of methane and small quantities of other hydrocarbon gases and

The diesel LPG carrier *Traquair*, 7,230 tonnes dwt, built by Ferguson-Ailsa for Anchor Line ltd.   *Ferguson-Ailsa*

nitrogen. It is a clean burning and efficient fuel which has provided energy for industry and the consumer for more than 200 years. Being a relatively inexpensive fuel it is not surprising that worldwide demand for gas has increased from about 10 trillion cubic feet per year in the 1950s to 44 trillion cubic feet in 1977.

Initially, natural gas associated with oil was produced and supplied to markets near the point of production. As demand increased new and larger sources of non-associated gas were discovered and developed, so this second generation of gas fields provides most of the current production. But these sources are more remote from the urban and industrial markets which they serve. Then in the 1960s production and consumption increased beyond the rate of growth of nearby reserves, forcing the major consuming nations

One of the products carried by chemical carriers is ethylene; this IHI-built ethylene carrier is the 456 dwt *Ethylene Unakami. IHI*

The *Genkai Maru*, a 49,997 tonnes dwt LPG carrier built by IHI for the Idemitsu Tanker Co Ltd and completed in 1980.   *IHI*

The Kawasaki-built LPG carrier *Sun River*, which has a capacity of 75,000cu m.   *Kawasaki*

to consider importing natural gas from fields located overseas. For a number of reasons, including economics, pipelines were precluded as a means of shipment across oceans, so this brought about a new breed of ship transportation — the LNG carrier.

Due to reasons of transport and economy the gas is liquefied at the loading terminal prior to shipment, reducing its volume by a factor of about 600. The LNG is loaded aboard ship at the appropriate liquefying temperature and transported in specially constructed tanks at a vapour pressure slightly above atmospheric pressure. At the discharge terminal the LNG is stored in cryogenic tanks on shore and later heated, vaporised and injected in the gas distribution system.

The first ever liquified natural gas cargo carried by an ocean-going ship was on the *Methane Pioneer* (later renamed *Aristotle*) which successfully transported LNG from Lake Charles, Louisianna to Canvey Island on 20 February 1959. The *Methane Pioneer* was a converted dry cargo ship and was fitted with five self-supporting aluminium tanks fitted into two holds internally insulated with a balsa system.

Before the *Methane Pioneer* made its epic journey there had been a number of studies and experiments to determine practical and safe ways to ship LNG. One study in 1951 had been initiated to investigate the movement of natural gas as a liquid in the USA, while proposals were formulated to transport gas from the Middle East, either by pipeline or as LNG at sea. Independent research was carried out to study the possibilities of adapting existing ship technology by fitting internal insulation. Study was made on two types of insulation material: blown plastic foams such as Styrofoam, and woods as such as cork and balsa.

Fleets of 125,000cu m LNG carriers are now the rule rather than the exception. The *LNG Aquarius* was one of eight such carriers specially built for charter by Burma to transport LNG from Indonesia to Japan.

Another study by Gaz de France stimulated LNG development further. In the late 1950s it carried out a study on the possibility of moving natural gas from Salaca into France and decided that marine transportation was the most economical method of doing this. An experiment then began with a Liberty ship. The rules of the Classification Societies had already kept pace with LNG development, and one important feature that influenced new designs was the requirement of a secondary barrier.

One landmark in the development of LNG shipping was when the *Methane Princess* on 12 October 1964 landed the initial delivery of a 15-year 100 million cubic feet per day shipment. During the following decade several other moderately-sized transportation schemes were implemented, but it was not until the start of the Shell 500 million cubic feet per day Brunei to Japan project that the marine community realised the importance of large-scale movement of LNG over long distances. The future energy requirements of the world now ensure that there will be an increasing demand for LNG. Several projects calling for the delivery of thousands of millions of cubic feet have been implemented in the past few years, while others are being planned. LNG ships will thus continue to play an important role in marine transportation in coming years, but their design will be more toward technological refinement rather than major technological breakthroughs. Ships will become larger, possibly faster, and certainly more numerous.

Early LNG ships were determined by the state of the art and project size, but recent LNG projects have reached the staggering proportions where fleets of 125,000cu m ships are the rule rather than the exception. The LNG carrier is a large, fast vessel of light draught, highly powered and usually single-screw. In the early days moderate-sized vessels were designed with conventional hull forms, but these could only be used up to a certain ill-defined maximum ship size and power. The problem of propeller-induced vibration as encountered in single-screw hulls of large LNG vessel type configuration fostered innovation in the form of open type sterns which provide nearly ideal hydrodynamic conditions in way of a single-screw propeller.

Of prime consideration in LNG ships is the tanks. LNG in a vessel is carried under cryogenic conditions in a series of specially designed tanks with primary and secondary barriers, and with insulation as protection. These cargo containment systems may be broken down into two broad classes; self-supporting tanks and membrane tanks. The above broad categories can be broken down again into five types of general containment systems: free-standing prismatic and cylindrical; free-standing spherical; membrane; semi-membrane; and integrated tanks. In what follows certain major containment designs are described.

Self-supporting or free-standing tanks are capable of withstanding all design loads without aid from the ship's structure. These tanks are considerably more massive than membrane tanks and heavy lift facilities are required either at the tank construction site or the shipyard to lift the tanks into the hull. Construction of the tanks in a facility separate from the shipyard is an advantage of a containment system featuring self-supporting tanks; this means tank construction can proceed independently of ship construction.

With membrane tanks the cargo is contained in a membrane insulation system which is supported by the hull structure. The membrane tanks have no internal structure, and thus, no internal strength of their own. They must be constructed totally within a completed hull. The membrane system has considerably less tank mass than a self-supporting system but the installation is usually more labour intensive and must be accomplished subsequent to hull construction, on board the vessel.

Nearly all efforts toward the design of containment systems were directed toward the free-standing tank. Prismatic systems received the wider acceptance, utilising more efficiently the volume encompassed by the containment envelope. The Conch prismatic and associated insulation system is the result of the revolutionary development of the system as developed for the *Methane Pioneer* (now *Aristotle*), *Methane Princess* and *Methane Progress*, which evolved from tests carried out on the barge *Methane*. The Conch free-standing system as initially installed in the *Methane Pioneer*, in essence consists of five aluminium tanks stiffened by horizontal angles, with diagonal ties and horiztonal ties connecting the sides of the tanks. The insulation system consists of laminated balsa panels faced on the inner surface with sugar maple plywood and on the back with Douglas fir pine. The system used in the *Methane Princess* and *Methane Progress* was a development of the earlier Conch system, with an escalation of the tanks and a centreline bulkhead added. Substantial changes were made to the insulation system, although the basic concept of balsa panels and a plywood secondary barrier was maintained.

Spherical free-standing tanks were originally proposed to provide a primary LNG containment system which did not require a secondary barrier, because it was claimed that the spherical tank was essentially a pressure vessel, not requiring any emergency containment capability. Subsequent regulatory action stated that for certain cases a partial secondary barrier in the form of a drip tray was to be provided, with a splash barrier insulation so that LNG leakage into the primary could not impinge directly upon the ship's structure. All spherical designs — similar or otherwise

The 129,000cu m Kawasaki-built *Golan Spirit*. *Kawasaki*

— possess the same advantages and disadvantages over other forms of LNG containment. The large volume of sphere above the main deck produces a ship which is considered by some to be of less than optimum configuration for operational handiness.

One example of a free-standing tank system is the Kvaerner-Moss system, which consists of a sphere supported by a cylindrical skirt attached at its top to a forged or extruded ring at the tank equator, and at the bottom to the ship's structure. The cylindrical skirt, welded to the equatorial ring and to the ship's structure, is stiffened, whereas the tank itself is not. Several insulation techniques have been used or proposed. One technique is the use of panels of rigid expanded polystyrene reinforced with glass fibre mesh and attached to the exterior of the tank and the upper portion of the cylindrical support skin. A second technique employs a continuous expanded polystyrene section, reinforced with fibrous glass mesh and applied automatically to the tank surface in a spiral manner. A third technique utilises multiple layers of foamed polyurethane attached to the tank and skirt with studs then sealed with an elastometric vapour barrier.

Another free-standing spherical tank system is the Technigraz system, which is similar in concept but much different in detail. Yet other systems of the type are the CBI (Chicago Bridge & Iron) free-standing spherical tank system and the Sener free-standing spherical containment system, which employs the unstiffened, analysible, leak-before-failure concept used by the spherical tanks described above and has insulation of polystyrene or polyurethane foam over its entire spherical surface and the upper part of the support skirt.

The development of the membrane tank, in which a thin metallic or other lining within an insulated hold replaces the heavy free-standing tank structure, was initially claimed to give substantial cost savings over other types of containment systems. Unfortunately, this is not universally valid, but the installation of membrane and insulation does interfere less with classic shipbuilding than do free-standing tanks.

The nature of the membrane tank makes it extremely difficult, if not impossible, to analyse structurally, and all elements have to be subjected to comprehensive testing programmes involving thermal properties and fatigue performance, the latter covering cyclic temperatures and pressure tests, as well as producing ship deflection in a heavy seaway. Two successful membrane systems are those of Technigraz and Gaz Transport. The Technigraz membrane originated in work done during the late 1950s in Norway, and the present formation of waffled stainless steel membrane primary barrier, balsa insulation and plywood secondary barrier is the outgrowth of the formation of Conch Ocean Ltd in 1967 by Conch International Methane Ltd and Gazocean SA.

The Technigraz system consists — from ship's structure inwards — of insulation, secondary barrier, additional insulation and primary barrier. Insulation panels consisting of laminated balsa layers faced with Douglas fir pine on the warm side, and maple plywood on the cold side which are attached to the grounds. The Gaz Transport system consists — from ship's structure inwards towards cargo — of secondary insulation and secondary barrier, primary insulation and primary barrier. The insulation layers and barriers are virtually identical and insulation consists of a multitude of perlite-filled plywood boxes about a metre long, 400mm wide and 200mm thick, with Invar being chosen for the barriers.

The main disadvantages associated with the free-standing and membrane tanks are claimed to be loss of cubic capacity, a large amount of structural weight, with welded footage in the case of the former, and a complex insulation and painstaking welding and inspection in the case of the latter. To embody the advantage of each type, while eradicating the disadvantages, the semi-membrane tank was designed. It is, in fact, a membrane tank in which the thickness of the primary barrier approaches that of a free-standing tank. In a semi-membrane tank the primary barrier is almost completely unattached to the insulation and ship structure. In the loaded condition hydrostatic head and vapour pressure above the cargo surface will hold the primary barrier in position. In ballast, vapour pressure alone must be depended upon, and it appears that frequent spraying of LNG may be required to keep the primary barrier from warming and expanding.

One system based on the semi-membrane tank system is the IHI Flat Tank System, which allows a reduced secondary barrier owing to its high reliability stemming from its structural design. The tank is composed of eight flat walls and corners, each sectional form of which consists of a special fair curve. The contraction of the tank at low temperature and the deflection of the tank walls due to liquid pressure and additional acceleration can be fully absorbed by the transformation of the curved edges.

Several aerospace companies in the United States

have developed containment systems based on their experience and expertise acquired through the aerospace programme. In general, these 'integrated tank' systems, as they are called, might be termed 'membrane-less membrane tanks'. All the designs possess one common feature in that the tanks are built without the metallic liners which form the principal feature of the Gaz Transport and Technigraz membrane tanks.

In the carriage of any dangerous commodity safety must be of primary concern. LNG is a remarkably docile liquid provided the conditions of transport and storage remain normal, but can become lethal when these are radically altered, such as tank rupture or ship collision. One such tragic case was the Cleveland LNG disaster in 1944, which occurred in the midst of a populated area and resulted in heavy loss of life and property.

Conditions of safety will include wheelhouse visibility, liquid sloshing and boil-off of liquid. One study mentions an average value of 1.25 ship lengths as acceptable visibility over the ship's bow, but for the LNG ships the frequently counteractive constraints (not least being the excessive freeboard and long deck length) make this condition difficult to achieve. Liquid sloshing in tanks subjected to the motions of a ship at sea produces dynamic loads on the tank structure. Early LNG ships were of such size that sloshing was not a critical factor in design, and it was not until the first large membrane tank ships, *Polar Alaska* and *Arctic Tokyo*, came into service that the effect of sloshing came to be realised. Not only may liquid sloshing preclude the carriage of cooldown LNG while the ship is in ballast, but the ability of a ship to carry partial cargoes may be severely limited.

LNG is a continuously boiling liquid under conditions encountered in storage tanks on ships and ashore. In order to prevent dangerous pressure build-up some controlled means of disposal of boil-off vapour must be employed. At shore installations this is accomplished in simple fashion; large volumes of boiled-off and displaced vapour produced during loading operations are used as fuel then returned to the liquefication cycle, or flared. Afloat, the disposal of vapour can be somewhat more difficult. In the earliest days of LNG transport by sea, boiled off vapour was simply vented to the atmosphere. This caused the loss of several millions of BTUs-worth of energy. Recent regulatory directives have prohibited normal venting of vapour within some harbours and several schemes for the disposal of unusable boil-off vapour have been proposed. The steam dump system is most frequently chosen; vapour continues to be burned in the boilers and excessive steam is directed into the condenser, which must be of sufficient size to handle the load produced by vapour burned at the maximum boil-off rate. Yet another system is to reliquefy the LNG by means of a special refrigerating compressor.

Considering some recent LNG ships, tank containment systems and innovative designs — the *Lucian* was built by Moss Rosenberg as a multi-purpose liquefied gas carrier, being one of two 29,000cu m combined LNG/Ethylene/LPG carriers built and delivered in 1973-4. She was the first ever ship to carry LNG at sea in spherical tanks and was originally fitted with a 20,000bhp General Electric gas turbine to enable the LNG boil-off to be used for propulsive power. The first US-built LNG carrier, the *Aquarius*, was built by General Dynamics Corporation at its Quincy yard, Massachusetts, and was launched in May 1977. The first of a number of vessels of this class, it was chartered by the US owners to Burmah and operated under American crews sailing under the American flag. The vessel is able to carry 125,000cu m of LNG and was installed with a General Electric steam turbine plant, while its five 850-ton spheres were handled and positioned on board by the giant Goliath crane at the Quincy yard.

Considering tank containment systems, the first Moss-Rosenberg spherical tank system to be installed was in the LNG carrier *Lady Norman*, which was delivered in 1974. The first gas carrier to use the Sener spherical LNG containment system, the 5,000cu m

Aluminium LNG tanks under construction. *Moss Rosenberg*

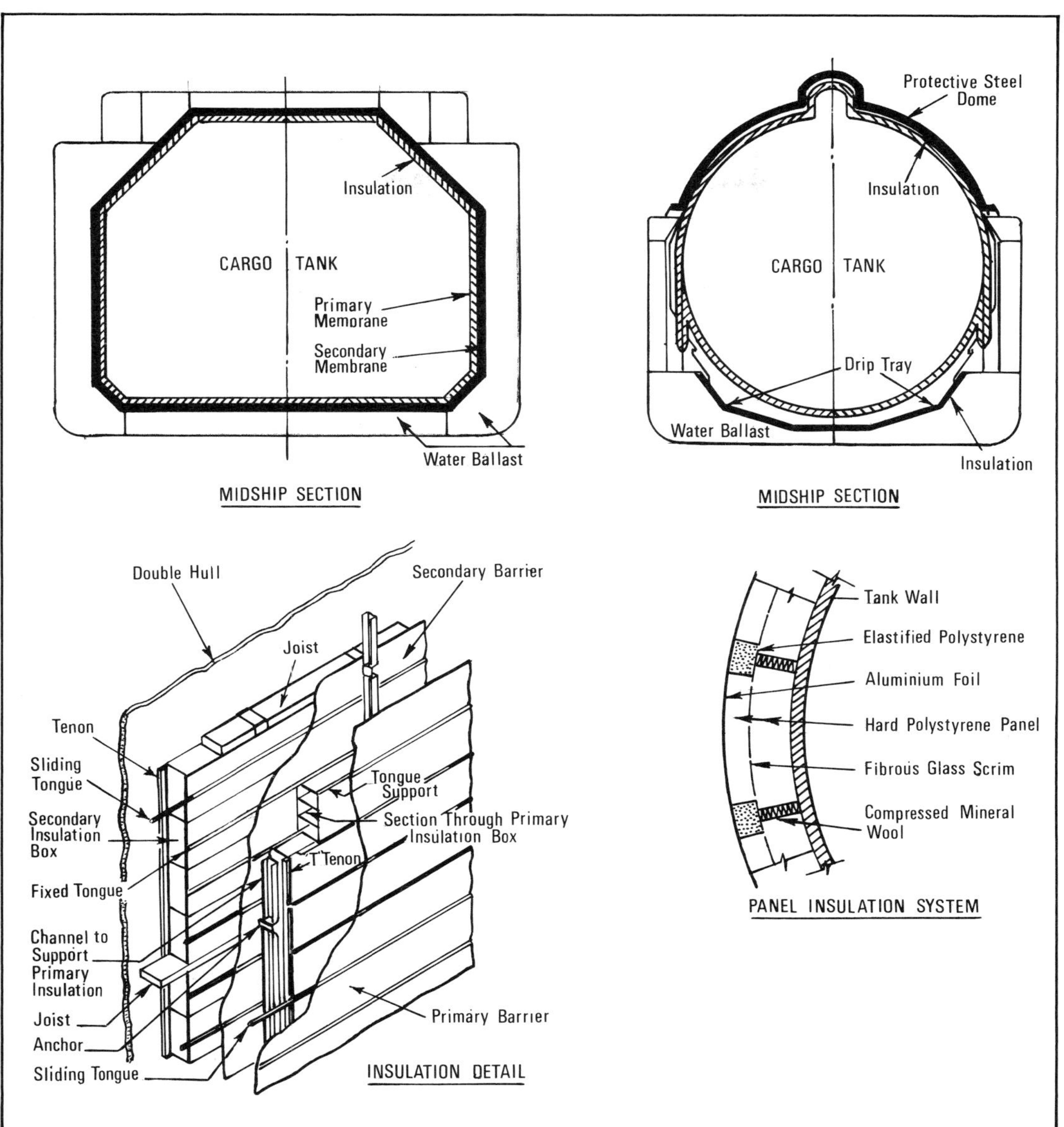

Cargo tanks for LNG carriers. Left: Midship section and insulation detail for free standing Gas-Transport Membrane Containment System. Above: Midship section and insulation detail for free standing spherical containment system.

Sant Jordi, was delivered in 1977, being designed to carry LNG, ethylene or LPG. The Technigraz membrane containment system, which has already been installed in about a dozen methane carriers around the world, employs a corrugated stainless steel primary barrier and a load bearing insulation system. Improved materials and fabrication techniques were introduced for the Mark III system, which for insulation has a bonded sandwich of plywood and rigid closed-cellular expanded foam, with an integrated secondary barrier of Triplex, a composite of aluminium foil and two layers of glass cloth. It was to be installed in a proposed 130,000cu m LNG carrier which an NKK team was attempting to market in Europe in 1979.

In terms of innovative designs, Mitsubishi has a 125,000cu m LNG carrier which offers reliability, economy and safety. It is based on the design concept called 'small leak protection system', which has been proven not only in theory but also by the excellent performance of long term operations. Finally, there is a design for a concrete LNG carrier which is further mentioned in the chapter on miscellaneous ships.

6

Bulk, Ore and Car Carriers

Bulk and ore carriers are specifically designed for the carriage of cargoes such as ore, grain, cement, sugar, coal, etc. The bulk sugar carrier is a development of recent years; the bulk ore carrier is usually a large ship with engines aft. A number of multi-purpose ships such as combination carriers have evolved since World War 2 to meet varying demands, and these will be discussed where applicable. The pure car carrier (PCC) was born out of bulk carrier trade and experience in the market, and has a legitimate place in this chapter. The gas carrier, being a complex and very specialised ship, has a separate chapter of its own.

The general bulk carrier has a double bottom, hopper sides and deck wing tanks. These tanks have been used for the carriage of light grain cargoes as well as water ballast. A typical bulk carrier will have a clear deck, machinery aft and large hatches to facilitate loading and discharge of cargo. The universal bulk carrier, patented by the MacGregor International Organisation, was a more refined form of bulk carrier offering a very flexible range of cargo storage solutions, taking ore, grain and coal cargoes.

The bulk carrier comes in a range of sizes, reflecting the various lengths of voyages and size of cargo flows. In the 100,000 tons dwt category are the iron and ore carriers, used for long voyages. Coal is moved in somewhat smaller vessels, usually of 50-70,000 dwt but sometimes up to 100,000 tons. Grain tends to move in ships of 50-60,000 dwt or less. The size of the bulk

carrier has steadily increased over the years and ore carriers have reached 150,000 dwt, while many oil/ore carriers top 200,000 dwt. In fact, a survey conducted in 1974 showed that less than one-sixth of the seaborne trade in the five main bulk commodities was transported by bulk carriers over 20,000 dwt in 1960: by the end of the decade this fleet was responsible for about 75% of bulk tonnage.

There are also bulk/ore carriers and one such vessel is the bulk/ore carrier *Awobasan Maru*, 138,655 tonnes dwt, built by IHI and completed in 1981.

The modern car carrier has a considerable number of decks — as much as 12 or 13 in some cases — which give it a very slab-sided or rectangular profile. One form of loading and unloading is by access through a stern quarter ramp and as many as 6,000 cars can be transported. An important requirement of design is high speed, which can be as much as 20kts.

The large bulk carrier originated as an ore carrier in the Great Lakes at the beginning of the century. In the late 1940s/early 1950s bulk carriers began to take over such cargoes as coal, ore, grain and timber from the 'tweendeck' cargo ships and since then the phenomenal growth in the world's bulk carrier fleet has been the single most important development in the dry bulk market. Historically, Japan has dominated the dry bulk market and it is predicted that its share of world seaborne trade in dry bulk commodities will remain substantial in the future.

The specialised bulk carrier is designed primarily to carry the maximum possible volume on a specific

The 1967-built *Grafton*. *Real Photos*

voyage, but with little or no prospect of a full load on the return voyage. With an increasing need to be more profitable, designers attempted to introduce versatility and flexibility, resulting in a number of conversions, new designs and multi-purpose ships of various types. Neo-bulk cargoes such as forest products, steel products, motor cars and even containers are carried. Containers were introduced almost by accident into the bulk carrier market when it was realised that the wide open decks of forest carriers — already designed to handle unitised cargoes — were perfect for the standard containers.

With the rapid expansion of the car exporting trades around the world — particularly out of Japan — bulk carriers found a new role for their employment. In the 1960s cars were being transported either in converted bulk carriers or in 'car bulkers', which to all intents and purposes were bulk carrier designs modified to enable ramp loading of cars on to the weather deck and internal deck distribution by lift systems. These early vessels could carry a maximum of about 1,200 cars. The last 12 years or so has seen the evolution of the PCC, the first one, being built in 1970 and having a capacity of 2,000 cars. By 1974 the world's largest PCC of the time had a capacity of 6,000 cars, which seems about the optimum size for this type of vessel.

To look at some of the various types of bulk carriers and car carriers, among the largest and most interesting are the combination carriers, which are split into two groups: ore/oil carriers and ore/bulk/oil (OBO) carriers. The former can carry cargoes of oil or a dense dry cargo such as iron ore in its mix of tanks and gastight holds. It is almost invariably of considerable size, ranging above 200,000 dwt and even up to 280,000 dwt. The first of this type was the *G. George Harrison*, 14,305grt, designed to carry ore in side tanks and return with oil in centre compartments. A recent version is the giant 227,588 dwt ore/oil carrier *Berge Adria* which, together with her sister ship *Berge Brioni*, was built in Jugoslavia for Norwegian owners. The present world's largest is the 282,462 dwt *World Gala*.

OBOs have only gastight holds, which are able to take oil and carry grain and coal as well as ore. OBO carriers are typified by the 127,050 dwt *Angelic Blessing* and most are around 120,000 dwt, with some being smaller or larger. OBOs of less than 70,000 dwt

The *Widar*, built by Bohm + Voss and delivered in 1971, is a 78,954 dwt bulk carrier. *Blohm + Voss*

are rare, being too small for the tanker market. One of the larger OBO vessels is the IHI-built *Nippon Maru No 3* of 156,800 tonnes dwt.

Two notable limitations on bulk carriers — both relating to the vessel's breadth — have brought about the maximisation of dimensions. Ships of more than 22.8m breadth cannot enter the Great Lakes, while ships of more than 32.26m breadth cannot use the Panama Canal. These limitations have brought about the 'Panamax' bulk carrier of around 50-70,000 dwt for the Panama Canal and the 25-28,000 dwt ship to conform to the Great Lakes restrictions. Great interest has been shown in Panamax bulk carriers and one study in 1980 reported that 72 Panamax-sized bulk

Bulk and ore carriers come in a range of sizes, in the 100,000 dwt category being the iron ore carriers. The *Pioneer Maru*, built by IHI and completed in 1978, is a 129,829 tonnes dwt ore carrier. *IHI*

The *USA Maru*, built by IHI, is a 286,000 dwt ore/oil carrier.
IHI

carriers had been ordered in the first half of that year. One 72,150 dwt Panamax bulk carrier built by Sunderland Shipbuilders in 1976 for Jugoslavia, was of interest in that it was the first UK vessel built for that country in 30 years. A typical Panamax bulk carrier is the 60,992 dwt *Strategist*, delivered to her Liverpool owners T&J Harrison in 1975 by Burmeister & Wain.

The growing interest in Panamax economy carriers, as they are sometimes known, has centred on standard designs in recent years. For instance, there is a Burmeister & Wain economy Panamex type bulk carrier, and one such vessel was the *Hydrock*, built in 1980 and the second of a series for the Wheelock Marden maritime group.

Economic running has become prominent in bulk carrier design since the oil crisis, including the incorporation of energy-saving devices. One aspect of this is coal-fired power for ship propulsion, and orders for two 75,000 dwt bulk carriers powered by coal-fired

turbines were placed in 1980 with Mitsubishi Heavy Industries by the Australian National Line. Misubishi also has a most advanced fuel-saving very large bulk carrier (VLBC) design for a 207,000 dwt bulk carrier with two sets of slow-speed diesel engines as part of its energy-saving package. In 1981 the company signed a contract with Shinwas Kaiun Kaisha Ltd for the construction of a 207,000 dwt ore bulk carrier incorporating many greatly advanced energy-saving features.

Considering smaller bulk carriers, there is a need for carriers of up to 26,000 dwt or so — a popular size which can carry a host of cargoes such as iron ore, coal, grain and 'minor' bulks. Interest for standard designs in such sized vessels is also considerable and one popular-sized bulk carrier built in Japan in 1971 was the *Attica*, the first 21,500 dwt standard series Fortune ship. Developed by IHI, two other designs of standard cargo ships were the 'Freedom' and the 'Friendship' the whole being called the 'F' series. The first 'Friendship' type general open bulk carrier, the 22,464 dwt *Falcon*, was delivered in 1978. Another standard bulk carrier design in the range is Austin & Pickersgill's B26, of which the 26,000 dwt *Lynton Grange* for Houlder Bros was the seventh of the design and launched in 1976.

The IHI-built *Awobasan Maru* is a bulk/ore carrier of 138,655 tonnes dwt and was completed in 1981.   *IHI*

Other standard bulk carrier designs by A&P are the 30,000 dwt B30 and the 35,000 dwt B35.

In the mini-bulk carrier range there is an interesting type of vessel known as the 'Paragraph' ship. This sprang from the design boards of Appledore Shipbuilders in the 1970s and although classified as a bulk carrier, the type can also take general cargo and 20ft containers, as well as carrying grain, timber or coal. What are Paragraph ships? Well, in simple terms the design maximises the deadweight tonnage under paragraphs in the Classification Society rules and regulations: in other words, optimum cargo carriage for the size of vessel. One Paragraph bulk carrier built by Appledore Shipbuilders was *Leslie Gault*, the first of a series of 1,599grt vessels handed over to its owners, Gallic Shipping in 1977.

Still with mini-bulk carriers, there is the 'Colne' class built by James W. Cook & Co (Wivenhoe) Ltd. These vessels, with their distinctive hard chine hulls, range from 600 dwt and reached a capacity of 1,550 dwt with three sister ships built in 1978, one of which was the *Belgrade*. A feature of these singledecker ships was their folding steel bulkheads, enabling them to trade in grain of high density, stowing to IMO requirements without the need to bag the grain.

Cement carriers are typified by the 38,400 dwt cement/bulk carrier *Guridi*, delivered in 1981. A smaller version is the 3,200grt self unloading bulk cement carrier *Golden Bay*, launched in 1979. Built for the Golden Bay Cement Co by Robb Caledon Shipbuilders, its cement handling system consists of aerated conveyors and screw pump machinery.

Forest products carriers have grown in recent years, a standard 29,000 dwt ship of around 1970 rising to 38-45,000 dwt in 1977. Further increase is not likely due to the constraints of the Panama Canal. This type of ship has squared-off holds to accommodate packaged timber, while the whole underdeck space is directly accessible to the ship's cranes. One such vessel is the 32,000 dwt bulk carrier *Thuleland*, first of two carriers designed to carry forest products and bulk cargoes in arctic waters without icebreaker assistance. In 1978 the world's first icebreaking bulk carrier *Arctic* was completed, having a double skin including a double bottom which extends to the fore and aft peak bulkheads and around the steering gear compartment.

Ro/ro facilities are sometimes incorporated in bulk carriers. Multi-purpose vessels of this type, designed to load ro/ro as well as bulk and oil cargoes, are designated as Bo-Ro ships. The founder of the Bo-Ro project was Capt B. W. Tornqvist and two such vessels of this type are the *Bellman* and *Taube*, a notable feature of their design being the distinctive trapezoidal form of their hull below the waterline.

Capt Tornqvist took a step further in this direction when in 1976 he introduced two ship designs for the carriage of containers, ro/ro freight and bulk cargoes. Known as the Bulkliner 2000 and Tankliner 2000, the

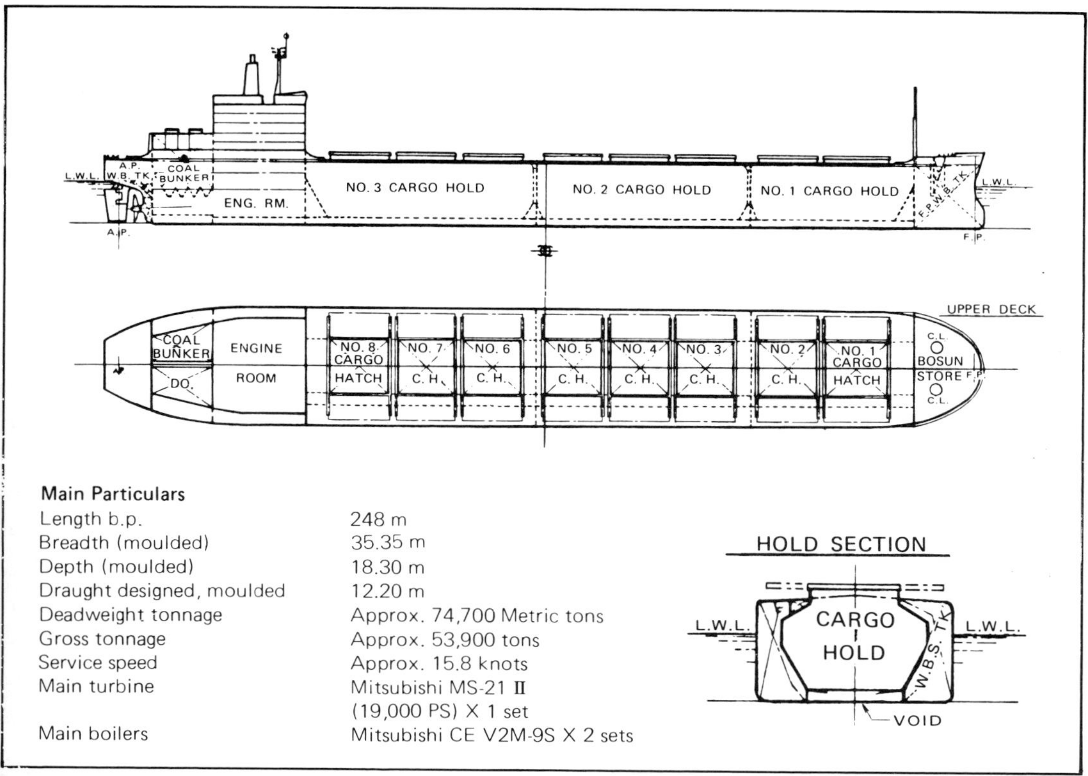

Main Particulars

Length b.p.	248 m
Breadth (moulded)	35.35 m
Depth (moulded)	18.30 m
Draught designed, moulded	12.20 m
Deadweight tonnage	Approx. 74,700 Metric tons
Gross tonnage	Approx. 53,900 tons
Service speed	Approx. 15.8 knots
Main turbine	Mitsubishi MS-21 II (19,000 PS) × 1 set
Main boilers	Mitsubishi CE V2M-9S × 2 sets

Diagram of Mitsubishi coal fired bulk carrier. *Mitsubishi*

The Ben Line bulk carrier *Benvorlich (V)* of 38,711 dwt.
Ben Line

The 4,412 tonnes dwt diesel bulk carrier *Zgorzelec*, built by
Ferguson-Ailsa Ltd for the Polish Steamship Co, is suitable for
worldwide trading and the carriage of timber deck cargoes.
This type of vessel has taken over cargoes from the
'tweendeck' cargo ship.   *Ferguson-Ailsa*

designs were basically for 268m long lift-on/lift-off
container and ro/ro car carriers with hold space for
either black oil products or dry bulk cargoes.

Bulk carriers that also carry cars need to be adapted,
and car decks have been designed which either
collapse to the sides of holds, stow on decks or are
hoistable when not required. One vessel that had
MacGregor Omega lightweight hoistable decks was the
Skaugran, a ship primarily designed to carry forest
products in semi-bulk form. The bulk carriers *Janega*,
Jacora and *Jalanta* were retrofitted with car decks in
1978, based on Norwegian technology. The basic
operating concept is the fitting of holds with large steel
plate temporary decks which, when the vessel is used
to haul cargo, are stacked in the vertical position
alongside the hold bulkheads. Yet another vessel that
carries cars as well as bulk cargoes is the 51,600 dwt
Aida, which has giant garages on deck for car shipments as well as holds for bulk cargo.

Taking a look at PCCs, the *Pacific Highway* is a car
carrier built by Kawasaki. In 1975 there saw the completion of the world's largest PCC at the time, the
16,000 dwt *Jinyu Maru*, which had a capacity for
6,000 cars. In 1976 the *don Carlos* was delivered to
her owners Wallenius Lines and had capacity for 4,950
cars on its 12 decks. In 1978 yet another world's
largest was launched, this time the 15,400 dwt car
carrier *Jinmei Maru*, which had 13 decks for the
carriage of 6,000 cars. Then came the *Madame
Butterfly* in 1981, the first of four 17,000 dwt car
carriers for Wallenius Lines and having 6,100 car
capacity. Built by Kockums in Sweden, these vessels
have 13 decks and a speed of nearly 20kts.

One typical OBO vessel is the IHI-built *Nippon Maru No 3* of
156,800 tonnes dwt.   *IHI*

The carriage of forest products is a growing trade. One country
involved in this trade is the USSR; pictured is the 'Mirni' type
timber carrier *Sofya Perovskaya*, 3,930 tonnes dwt.
Baltic Shipping Co

There is a need for bulk carriers of up to 26,000 dwt; a vessel in this range is the *Kopalnia Szombierki*, 16,500 tonnes dwt, built by Smith's Dock. *Smith's Dock*

The Kawasaki-built car carrier *Pacific Highway*. *Kawasaki*

The vehicle carrier *Grieg* (1972). *Real Photos*

7
Barge Carriers

The barge carrier concept seems to have had a pattern of development similar to that of containerisation, but incorporating certain major differences. Both ideas were conceived and developed in the USA in order to increase efficiency and reduce costs but unlike containerisation, which was initially developed on intra-US routes before reaching the international scene, the barge carrier had an immediate impact on international routes from the outset.

Although containerisation of cargoes (containers, lorries, flats and pallets) had been introduced, along with specialised ships to carry them, they still led to port delays and, thus, increased costs. Realisation began to dawn among certain naval architects and shipowers that what was needed was a separation of the ship as a motive unit from the hold as a carrying unit. From such thinking emerged the barge carrier concept.

The USA has a highly developed network of navigable rivers and naval architects in that country directed attention toward developing methods by which barges could become units for trans-oceanic journeys. At the same time designers and shipping companies in other countries were thinking on similar lines. Since then barge carrying technology has developed at an amazing pace, with only 10 years between serious design and a worldwide operating system.

Barge carrying vessels (BCVs) have now been in service for well over 10 years and there are several different types, most of them working the lift-on-lift-off system of loading barges over the stern. Some of the major systems are LASH (Lighter Aboard Ship), SeaBee, Bacat and the USSR Valmet system. LASH and SeaBee were largely introduced through the United States Government subsidy system and the majority of existing barge carrier systems are based in New Orleans, at the mouth of the Mississippi, where the LASH and

The *Doctor Lykes*, one of a series of barge carriers developed by Lykes Bros on the SeaBee concept. *Real Photos*

The TM barge carrier dockship *Baco-Liner 2*, built in 1980 and able to carry 12 lighters. *Sky Photos*

SeaBee designs evolved. Barge carrier services have proved to be outstandingly successful when linking two major river basins such as the Mississippi and the Rhine, but those based on the Pacific and Atlantic ports have not proved as profitable.

The LASH system is in widespread use on trade routes to most ports of the world, the first ship entering service in September 1969. This was the *Arcadia Forest*, the world's first BCV. The eight years succeeding this saw some 4,300 lighters carried on additional vessels to all continents. While general cargoes have mostly been carried, LASH lighters have also carried bulk grain and bulk ore concentrates.

The general design of the LASH ship is not much different from a conventional bulk carrier with a single deck, except that the foreship has been foreshortened by placing the bridge and accommodation superstructures well forward, with the machinery located as far aft as possible. It has a broad transom stern with a pair of heavy cantilevers projecting aft. These act as a docking area and crane runway for the massive crane which runs along the length of the ship. The crane lifts the lighters out of the water and stacks them in cells three high, similar to containers. The main deck has a series of hatches to allow for access of the lighters. Fin stabilisers have been fitted to a number of vessels to avoid damage to cargo. The barge carrying capacity of different classes of LASH vessels are 74, 83 and 89, respectively, Dimensions vary from 261-272m length

The TM barge carrier *Spruce*. *Sky Photos*

overall, 30.4-32.5m beam, and 10.7-12.4m loaded draught. The LASH vessels were originally designed as straight barge carriers but have undergone some developments. Recent versions of LASH vessels are designed to transport up to 40% of capacity in containers. The lighter (or barge) may be likened to a floating container, having characteristic dimensions of 18.8m length, 4.5m breadth and 4m depth, with a deadweight of 375 tons.

The SeaBee concept — which was originally an idea of Frank A. Nemec — was developed by Lykes Brothers Steamship Company in 1964. The company wished to develop a series of vessels that would represent a technological breakthrough in ocean development. Unlike the LASH carrier, with its series of holds, the SeaBee type vessel has three continuous decks. The engineroom is located aft under the lower deck and the bridge structure situated well forward, being supported clear of the upper deck by pillars. The principal dimensions are 267m length overall, 32.3m beam, 11.8m draught, and it has a speed of 19.5kts at maximum draught and 39,026 tons dwt, making it among the largest of common carrier freight vessels in the world.

The barges on the SeaBee are loaded by a stern elevator housed on a raised poop deck then transferred to the three decks by wheeled transport. Each barge is of 840 tons dwt. The second generation of SeaBee ships is represented by two 37,850 tons dwt Finnish barge carriers which started a new service operating between the Black Sea, Middle East and South East Asia. The vessels have been designed around the new Soviet designed Danube-barges.

The Danish company Bacat Systems was responsible for the 2,600 dwt *Bacat I* project which led to the first barge-aboard-catamaran vessel which entered service between Hull, Middlesbrough and Rotterdam in March, 1974. It is designed for operation on coastwise short sea and inter-island services and also provides feeder services for long-haul deep sea carriers.

The Bacat system is based on the Bacat barge which is smaller than the LASH barge. It is a twin-hulled design closed at bow and open at the stern; ten 140 dwt barges are hoisted by a platform arrangement at stern then traversed by roller to their stowed position. The tunnel between the twin hulls can accommodate three 370 dwt LASH type barges which are floated into position then hydraulically locked into position to complete the hull contour.

Bacat II is a larger version of *Bacat I* and designed around the module of the LASH barge, being able to carry six such units in the tunnel and 10 on the upper deck. With slight modifications 20 Bacat II barges can be carried on the upper deck, such barges being a half module of the LASH barge. The vessel — which also incorporates the fitting of a container crane and adaption of the deck to carry up to 312 TEUs in lieu of cargos — is designed for similar service to Bacat I.

Another unique development of BCVs came with the design of the *Capricorn Carrier* in 1976. From the beginning it was designed as a multi-purpose combination ro/ro vessel, barge carrier and container ship. The basic design included a stern ramp for ro/ro, a bow door allowing LASH barges to be floated in and out of a flooded hold, and gantry crane on deck to handle con-

tainers. Barges are handled by a float-in/float-out (flo/flo) system through vertically hinged bow doors, and carried in a single tier in the hold, being pushed into position by the vessel's own tug boat. Once the bow doors are closed the hold is pumped dry, leaving the barges resting on the tank top. Ro/ro cargoes are handled over the stern ramp and stowed on the upper deck. Like Bacat, Capricorn was originally designed around the module of the LASH barge and for operation on short sea, inter-island and coastal routes, as well as being able to provide a feeder service for deep sea carriers. Depending on vessel size, a varying number of barges of different sizes can be carried in the hold. It can also be readily adapted to handle Becat II, LASH, SeaBee or Valmet size barges as well as standard Mississippi and Danube Sea barges.

Two other multi-purpose carriers are *Baco 1* and *2* which have dispensed with the heavy barge lifting cranes. They use a flo/flo system to carry in a dock 12 Baco barges each of 800 tons dwt and 500 TEUs stored entirely on deck; hence the name, derived from barge and container. Compatability with other barge systems is afforded as each ship can alternatively carry 14 LASH barges or four Europa lighters.

The Valmet system is based on the SeaBee design of hoisting and stowing by means of a lift at stern then traversing them to their stowage position, but the barges are larger and have a dwt capacity nearly three times greater than LASH barges. They are identical with the Danube Sea barge, which is a half module of the Europa II barge. The BCV is designed to carry 26 of these barges and can also carry containers in lieu or, with special arrangements, other kinds of cargo, heavy lifts, etc. If LASH barges are used, up to a total of 52 can be carried.

A new adaptation in BCV design is *Trimariner* or *Ocean Lift*, which is designed to handle very large barges for long haul deep sea voyages. The vessel is designed on the float-dock principle, a refinement of

The TM barge carrier dockship *Condock II* with a TEH capacity of 383 or three lighters; built in 1979. *Sky Photos*

the Landing Ship Dock (LSD) concept. The open dock area is 185m long, 25m wide and 5m draught when the ship is floating down to its maximum loading draught of 14m. The basic design carries three barges 61m long and 24m beam, and can also be used to carry a greater number of smaller-sized barges in a single tier. It can be readily adapted or converted to other uses, such as ro/ro or carriage of dry bulk cargoes.

Other systems worth mentioning include the European Barge Carrier System (EBCS), a concept developed by Blohm + Voss, and an apparent answer to the US LASH system; Thyssen, a method similar to the Capricorn Carrier and designed to carry 24 LASH barges; Podule, a flo/flo system through a bow door; Dorads, a rather complex system somewhat similar to Trimariner.

Ocean-going barges — while still rare in conventional shipping operations — have been around for a long time as part of the marine transportation scene. In certain parts of the world such as America barges are more attractive than conventional shipping operations for certain trades, while large barges are common in the offshore industry because few conventional vessels are capable of transporting giant modules in excess of 2,000 tons.

Barge types generally fall into 11 classifications: flat deck, covered, bulk cement, rail, bulk carriers, special purpose, chip, chemical, tanker, log and submersible. It is not uncommon to find barges that are combinations of two or more of these types, such as rail or covered barges which can also carry bulk liquid chemicals. Ro/ro facilities have also be incorporated on certain barges. The main advantage of a towed barge system is that it requires a relatively small crew to operate the tug and even less for the barge. Another attraction is that a barge is of relatively simple construction and easy to

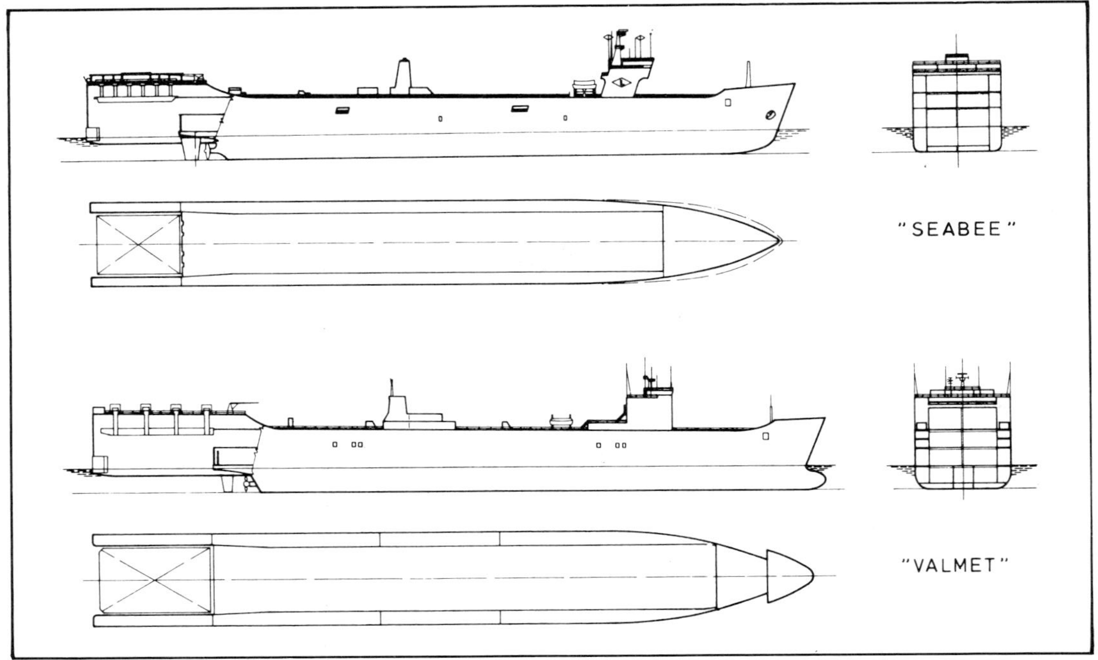

Comparison drawings of Valmet and the original SeaBee designs.

operate and maintain. Tugs, while being more expensive, can be multi-purpose and thus employed on other tasks when not in operation with the barge.

While barge transportation over long distances is not common in Europe, the Americans have always been firm advocates of tug/barge systems and employ them on liner services around the US coastline. One American company, the Crowley Maritime Corporation, laid tracks on some of their flat-topped barges and were able to transport rail cars on these Hydra-Train barges, as they were called, using the ro/ro principle. Following this experience, it built double-deck barges and furthering the idea, triple-decked barges.

One of the rare pure barging ventures outside US territorial waters is the EAST Line which has two triple-decked barges, *Arab Falcon* and *Arab Hawk*, which operate from France to Saudi Arabia and are handled by the multi-purpose tugs *Gladiator* and *Ranger*.

An alternative to the conventional tug/barge system is the Integrated Tug/Barge (ITB) concept, which is largely a feature of the North American coastal and

Great Lakes trades, where it developed from the widespread practice of towing barges in line. When pushing barges, the speed is not restricted by waterline length of the tug as it is when towing. US regulations also allow smaller crews than those of conventional ships of similar deadweight.

Systems for linking the tug and barge vary according to the degree of restraint imposed on relative motion between the vessels and the sea state at which they operate. The two types that emerge are the rigid and non-rigid type, the latter being restricted principally to coastal operations.

One concept of the rigid type is the Murvicker II Rigid Tug-Barge System whose tug/barge combination has the lines and seagoing qualities of a conventional vessel. The tug is seated in a deep notch in the barge and is seaworthy and manoeuvrable when acting on its own. The two units are held together by a hydraulically driven screw jack which engages with a vertical anchor pin in the barge.

An ITB that has been in service since 1977 is the *Valerie F*, which is of the basic patented Ingram/Breit design and has a deadweight of 28,000 tons with a service speed of 15kts. The tug, when mated in the barge's stern notch, rests on wooden blocks on the notch bottom and is locked at deck level through a system of wedges and a hydraulic connector. The tug-barge connector, a hydraulic cylinder at deck level, locks the tug in the secured position.

Five SeaBee barge units on the Mississippi River being pushed by one of the standard pusher tugs that operate on all American waterways. Two SeaBee barges are equivalent to one Mississippi River barge.

8
Container Ships

A container ship is a cargo ship specially designed and built for the carriage of cargo in prepacked containers. This leads to efficiency in stowage and the removal of much of the danger of the cargo shifting during heavy weather at sea. The modern practice is to carry additional containers stowed on deck, sometimes as many as three deep, although this has the adverse effect of reducing metacentric height. A number of vessels have been built with ro/ro and other facilities as well as container handling, but this chapter will generally concentrate on the pure container vessel.

Considering the palletisation aspects of container ships, the majority of containers are designed for general dry cargo but some specialised units can take liquid or powder cargoes, while some are refrigerated. Specially designed road vehicles, railway wagons, ships and dockside equipment handle units in a co-ordinated way. The container is now generally defined as a purpose-built and relatively long-lived unit of transport equipment, strong enough effectively to confine and contain its contents during repeated transits. Additionally, it is specifically designed for transit by more than one mode of transport and equipped with universally acceptable fittings to permit inter-modal handling.

Today's standard 20ft by 8ft by 8ft unit has its origins in the user-census conducted by the American Standards Association in 1961. The 20ft container was not readily accepted by the operators but eventually it became the universal module around which a wide range of hardware has been designed. There is also the 40ft by 8ft by 8ft container and to compare the size of container ships for whatever size container they have been designed, there is what is known as the 20ft equivalent unit (TEU).

Containers must be carried on board a ship on all decks, with the ratio of 20-footers to 40-footers being not more than 3:1. The movement of containers over the stern ramps is done in several forms; the TEUs are moved an athwartships attitude by forklift trucks or several are placed together on low 'bodies' in systems such as MAFI of LUF units.

Container construction has to be robust enough to withstand automatic handling, and a typically manufactured box is constructed of steel-framed alloy sheet with plywood lining. The floor is sufficiently strong to withstand the shock that arises from the entry of a heavy lift forklift truck. Although plywood/plastic and GRP have been used as cladding materials, alloy and steel are most commonly used. Internationally

recognised shipping bodies such as Lloyd's Register of Shipping undertake approval at both the design and production stages. The basic structure has to be inherently strong since a container at the bottom of a six-high stack can be subjected to loadings of 300/400,000lb.

Some of the first container ships were converted freighters, then more and more purpose-built ships went into service. Primarily a bulk carrier, the container ship has similar characteristics. Engines are located aft and there is a combined poop and bridge super-structure, a long uninterrupted deck and little or no forecastle. The cellular container ship is one which is fitted with guides to facilitate the positioning of containers and restrain them during the voyage.

Early container ships were equipped with gantry cranes for the unloading of their containers, but nowadays — as with the tanker and ore carrier — there are no cranes or other loading facilities as all loading and discharge is done by specialised dock equipment. Some container ships, however, do have transport or cranes which can operate the full length of deck. As containerisation developed further so containers were installed on the purpose-built quaysides of the container terminals, which require much more space than the conventional harbour. A road and rail network is also necessary so that the boxes can arrive and leave quickly. For this, specially designed road vehicles and railway wagons handle the standard box units, which are of agreed international dimensions.

The advent of containerisation as a means of cargo carriage was brought about because analysis of the times for loading and unloading conventional cargo ships, and the costs involved, showed that they were becoming prohibitive. The solution lay in more mechanisation, using forklift trucks, utilisation of goods and so on. This brought about a new thinking in merchant ship design. One of the first steps in this direction was the introduction of time-independent sideports where cargo was passed from forklift trucks on the quay to forklift trucks on board. The unitisation of cargoes rapidly developed to the floor-to-floor system where cargoes were built up at the factory floor then shipped to their final destination as an unbroken unit.

The containerisation of cargo for carriage is not altogether new; as far back as Egyptian times the two-handled earthenware amphora were specifically designed to facilitate the carriage of wines and other liquids by man, pack animal or ship. Nowadays, this is

BEN
ELLERMAN
BENU310035 0
JCB
30
TASKERS
Z 26616
ACT Z 26616

Freightliner
BEN
ELLERMAN
ACT
ACT
SCANIA

Carriage of cargoes by containers over land and sea has revolutionised the marine industry in postwar years. As this sequence of four photographs show, machinery and other cargoes are loaded at a container terminal (*top left*), transported by road and/or rail to the docks (*top right*), and loaded on board ship (*left*) either between decks or on top of the main deck (*right*). *Ben Line*

The container ship *ACT2* of 1982.   *Real Photographs*

referred to as intermodalism and during the early years of this century such adaptability was shown by the 'lift' vans with which the Bowling Green Storage and Van Company offered a service linking Europe and the United States.

It is now well over 20 years since cargo containerisation as we now know it was introduced into the maritime industry. As a result, container ships have taken the place of general cargo ships and have become the mainstream of marine transportation of dry cargoes even having refrigerated facilities in certain vessels such as the *Willowbank*. Traditional methods have usually involved numerous crates of miscellaneous shapes and sizes, and carried by diverse means. With the development of the container ship a completely integrated system emerged, based on the use of standard units.

The container revolution as we know it started in the USA in the mid-1950s. Although no single person can really claim to be its sole originator, Malcolm McLean, a trucker and creator of Sea-Land, can be considered the motivating force behind its inception. He started shipping operations in 1955, first converting T2 tankers to accept containers. The first big ship to be converted was the *Alema* in 1956. The next year saw the conversion of the C2 vessel *Gateway City*, as the world's first container ship.

The North Atlantic was the first major deep-sea route to change from conventional break-bulk shipping to containers, the ball being set rolling when the aptly named Sea-Land Services previously mentioned commenced operations between the US east coast and Europe. In 1966 came the first transatlantic crossing of a container ship, 10 years after the beginning of maritime transport of containers in the USA. Today on the North Atlantic there are seven mainstream operators offering very comparable services and competing for cargo, and the whole container business has undergone an impressive growth, almost totally eradicating conventional cargo-carrying operations. As an example of this growth, in 1965 at the beginning of containerisation in Europe, there were some 50 ships with a capacity of more than 250 TEU; at the end of 1977 this figure approached 1,000.

Classifying transatlantic container ships by generation, the first generation vessels are less than 1,000 TEU; second generation ships (which mark the beginning of containerisation between Europe and Australia in 1969) have capacities of above 1,000 TEU. With transoceanic vessels, part of the shipping is carried out by 'feeder' vessels because of factors concerning their daily costs and dimensions.

Because the North Atlantic is one of the major containerisation trades in the world it is well worth taking a look at the operators and the growth of their fleets. In 1978 the seven operators divided into American and European ownership. Flying the US flag were Sea-Land, United States Lines and American Export Lines. A fourth company — Seatrain — used UK flag ships on long term charter. Atlantic Container Lines (ACL), Dart Containerline and Hapag-Lloyd represented the European contingent. A number of these companies have changed ownership since 1978.

Considering the growth of these companies' fleets, in general the Americans opted for converted vessels at the beginning while the Europeans chose new ships. In 1968 Hapag-Lloyd was the first European company to

The *Sea-Land MacLean* of 1971 showing a centre-island ship. Note weathering on starboard side.   *Real Photos*

Seatrain Lines' *Eurofreighter* of 1972.   *Real Photos*

put fully cellular ships (four of 728 TEU) on the North Atlantic route, including the *Alster Express* which was lengthened after five years service to boost her capacity by 50%. Two more new vessels came in 1972 and the original four were jumboised to just over 1,000 TEU while four 1,500 TEU ships were entering service in 1978/9.

Just before Hapag-Lloyd's cellular ships entered service the United States Lines introduced the first of a series of eight 1,300 TEU vessels and by 1971 the whole fleet was in service. At the same time it converted eight conventional ships into 1,009 TEU cellular vessels to give it the finest fleet of any line. In its fleet is the *American Leader*.

Dart Containerline was a combine of a Belgian, British and Canadian company and ordered three 1,500 TEU ships that were delivered in 1970/71 and ranked among the largest at that time. A fourth ship of similar size joined them in 1978. There was amazement in the industry when Seatrain commissioned four 27kts 1,920 TEU ships in 1970/72. These ships were powered by Pratt & Whitney gas turbines.

Another surprise for the industry was when Sea-Land — which was bought in 1961 by the Tobacco giant, Reynolds — decided to replace its old ships in the North Atlantic and ordered eight 33kts ships, including the *Sea-Land Market*, which were larger than any vessels on other lines, and able to carry 896 of Sea-Land's unique 35ft containers with 200 40-footers in addition. American Export Lines employed converted tonnage at first, although purpose-built 1,070 TEU vessels followed in due course.

ACL built ro/ro capacity into its first four ships, which were delivered in 1967. Six other ships followed quickly to make a fleet of 10 ships with a mix of ro/ro and container capacity by the end of 1970. Two of the ACL fleet are the *Atlantic Span* and *Atlantic Conveyor*, the latter being famous for its participation and sinking during the Falkland Islands conflict.

Looking at some landmarks in container ship design, construction and services, the world's largest and fastest refrigerated container ship of the time, the *Remuera*, was completed by Swan Hunters Shipbuilders for P&O in 1973. The present world's largest container ship is the *Kurama Maru*, at 43,476 dwt and 2,228 TEU. The 'Liverpool' class container ships which entered into the Europe-Far East container ship service in 1972, were designed from the start not to mix containers with any other types of cargo. Three years after their entry it was found that damage to containers was negligible, in addition to other advantageous features.

The first IHI container ship built for export was the 39,000grt *Svendborg Maersk*, which was delivered to its Danish owners in 1974. Other IHI-built container ships are the 30.007grt *Pacific Arrow* and the 30.323grt *Neptune Diamond*, completed in 1979. Also from Japan is the ro/ro and lo/lo container ship *Australian Emblem*, built by Kawasaki. Another container ship by the company is the high-speed vessel *Seven Seas Bridge*. The first container ship to be operated by Japanese shipping companies on a regular basis between the Far East and New Zealand entered service in 1976. This was the 29.194 dwt *Godwit*, with a capacity of 1,466 containers, including 34 reefer units. That same year the 31,000 dwt *Neptune Pearl* joined Neptune Lines' Far East Europe service, while

The refrigerated container ship *Willowbank*, 16,300 tonnes dwt, built by Smith's Dock for the Bank & Saville Line. *Smith's Dock Co*

the 17,500 dwt *Manchester Vanguard*, first of two 160m cellular container ships built by Smith's Dock for Manchester Lines, was launched.

The first of a number of short-sea container vessels, the 2,213 dwt *Bell Rover*, was delivered to its owners, the short-sea container shipping specialists Bell Lines, in 1977. The vessel was designed primarily to serve the company's Irish and Continental trade. Again in 1977, the *Table Bay* was built for OCL, the first of nine vessels for the South Africa-Europe Container Consortium. It entered service that year, but just before this OCL also received the first of two reefer container ships, the *Resolution Bay*, claimed to be the world's largest reefer ship at the time. It had a capacity of 1,950 TEU, including 1,223 insulated refrigerated units. Also in the OCL fleet are the *Moreton Bay* and *Discovery Bay*, both of which underwent a major conversion from steam turbine to slow-speed diesel at Govan's Shipbuilders.

Three ships that sail under the Ben Line Containerships flag are the *Benalder*, *Benavon* and *City of Edinburgh*. With a capacity of 3,032 TEU, these 75,596 tonnes dwt identical vessels are claimed to be among the largest and most efficient of their type afloat and have a service speed of 23kts. BLC is a combined venture of Ben Line and Ellerman Lines.

On a much smaller level, the 1,599grt *City of Plymouth*, the first of five small cellular container Paragraph ships for Ellerman City Liners, and built by Appledore Shipbuilders, underwent sea trials in 1978. These ships were designed specifically for an optimal size of operating economy, fuel and maintenance.

Finally, Russia has built up a large merchant fleet and has been seeking markets in all aspects of the shipping trade, including containerisation. Two of its container ships, owned by the Baltic Shipping Company, are the 6,447 dwt *Alexandr Prokofiev* and the 6,270 dwt 'Sestrorezk' type *Pioner Vyborga*.

The containership *Atlantic Conveyor*, part of the ACL fleet before its participation and sinking during the Falkland Islands conflict. It is seen here loaded with helicopters and other military equipment. *HMS Heron/Crown copyright*

Another Kawasaki building, the high speed *Seven Seas Bridge*.   Kawasaki

The Ben Line containership *City of Edinburgh* of 49,590 dwt. *Ben Line*

Ro/Ro Ships

The roll-on roll-off (ro/ro) vessel is the oldest of the specialised carriers, and its beginnings are not clear or distinct. Small ferries have been carrying wheeled vehicles across bodies of water for centuries. It was not until just before World War 2 that ships started to be loaded and unloaded through their sides and sterns. They were military vessels and called Landing Ship Tanks (LSTs) or landing craft. These vessels had a deadweight of 2,000 tons and were mostly built in the United States. The experience gained from such craft was used in developing the world's first ro/ro vessel, the USNS *Comet*, which was an ingenious ship for its time and launched in 1953 in the USA. This ship served as a prototype for later ro/ro vessels developed both sides of the Atlantic. In England an army officer, Colonel Buster, rebuilt some LSTs and started regular ferry services across the Channel. The success of his idea is marked by the fact that this particular trade is now dominated by ro/ro shipping.

What are the reasons for the success of ro/ro vessels? Well, they mostly stem from the fact that with properly designed equipment they can achieve higher handling rates and faster turn-around times than any other vessel. Cargo-handling absorbs a disproportionately large share of a vessel's operating costs and consequently shipowners have turned to ro/ro ships to reduce costs by minimising turn-around times and manpower requirements. Another reason is that ro/ro vessels are not so dependent on shore-based facilites as are other ships. They also require less quay space as loading and unloading are through the stern. Further reasons are as follows: each cargo unit on a ro/ro ship wheeled across the ramp is on an average heavier and larger than that for conventional or container ships, and no time or energy is wasted in lifting cargo over the ship's rail; once ashore, wheeled cargo can move freely away from congested port areas; the cargo does not have to be in uniform box sizes, while weight limitations are not as strict as in other cases; the exact location of each cargo unit within the vessel is not essential, while a continuous flow of cargo over ramps is possible; loading and discharge can be performed simultaneously without too much interference with each other; heavy equipment is not usually limited by 'lift' capacity.

But ro/ro vessels also have disadvantages. For instance, construction is expensive because of excessive cubage requirements of the ro/ro cargo. Technical difficulties cover such points as limitations in engineroom height, flatness and fullness of run aft, plus structural difficulties in constructing a wide open (horizontally) vessel. Other technical difficulties are the extremely heavy aft 'appendages' and supporting structures that cause vibration problems; the heavy deck construction to accommodate heavy vehicles; expensive and sophisticated cargo access ramp; transfer equipment; ventilation of cargo spaces, etc, and the expensive manoeuvrability units (bow and stern thrusters, controllable pitch propellers, etc) to allow for manoeuvrability in undeveloped ports. Finally, ro/ro vessels require reliable mooring and anchoring equip-

The 14,500 dwt *Ponce de Leon* launched in 1977. *Sun Shipbuilding*

ment, as such vessels cannot be allowed to move very much when cargo operations are going on.

Ro/ro vessels have been adopted as a solution in many parts of the world and a global look will be taken at their development and the role they play in marine transport and cargo carriage, beginning with North Sea operations. Ro/ro shipping really developed in the early 1960s and soon gained a stronghold in the North Sea. The popularity of passenger car ferries on short sea channel crossings, developments within the EEC and the establishment of containerisation on the deeper sea routes all provided a basis for this growth.

The *Bardic Ferry* was the first merchant ship designed for this ro/ro type of service, belonging to a company operating such services between England, Ireland and the Continent. The vehicles were loaded by stern ramp to the lower deck, and by a 20-ton crane to the upper deck. The first purely commercial ro/ro cargo vessel, *Somerset*, entered service for *Det Forande Dampskibs-Selskab* A/S (DFDS) in the Danish trade between Grimsby and Esbjerg in 1966.

DFDS has been an important operator in North Sea ro/ro services, and it is worth looking at some of its history and development in this area. The company dramatically showed its confidence in ro/ro ships when its flagship, *Dana Anglia*, entered service in 1978. It was Denmark's largest passenger ship at the time, with accommodation for 1,249 passengers and 470 cars. Regular sailings between Denmark and Britain have been a feature of the company's activities since its inception in 1866.

In 1966 the first step was taken that would lead to the complete transformation of the UK-Denmark freight service with the introduction of the *Suffolk*, on which

The MV *Dana Maxima*, 6,552 dwt, was specially designed to negotiate the lock at Grimsby. it operates on the DFDS UK-Denmark routes and its name implies maximum use is made of all available space for cargo carrying. *DFDS*

were loaded palletised crates of lager. For the movement of Danish bacon and other freight DFDS ordered two ro/ro ships, the *Somerset* and the *Stafford*, the first service using the *Somerset* being inaugurated in 1967. In the same year a new passenger ship, the *Winston Churchill*, was introduced on the Harwich-Esbjerg route.

At this stage DFDS became fully committed to the ro/ro concept and by the end of 1968 two-thirds of all Danish bacon was being transported in refrigerated trailers and carried on ro/ro vessels. The *Somerset* and the *Stafford* were lengthened to meet the growing demand, along with the *Suffolk* and another ship, the *Surrey*, which had been added to the fleet.

By the end of 1973 the switch to ro/ro services between Britain and Denmark was complete, and further vessels added to DFDS's fleet were the *Dana Anglia* previously mentioned, *Dana Futoria*, *Dana Gloria* and *Dana Maxima*, with the next development being a 12,000-ton passenger/car liner on the Tyne-Scandinavian routes in 1981, the new ship to be called the *Wellamo*.

Four generations of ro/ro freight vessels have been now tested in the North Sea, Channel and Irish Sea. The first generation were the LSTs, capable of accom-

Russia has entered the ro/ro market and one of its vessels, owned by the Baltic Shipping Co, is the 4,224 dwt ro/ro dry cargo ship *Mekhanik Tarasov*. *Baltic Shipping Co*

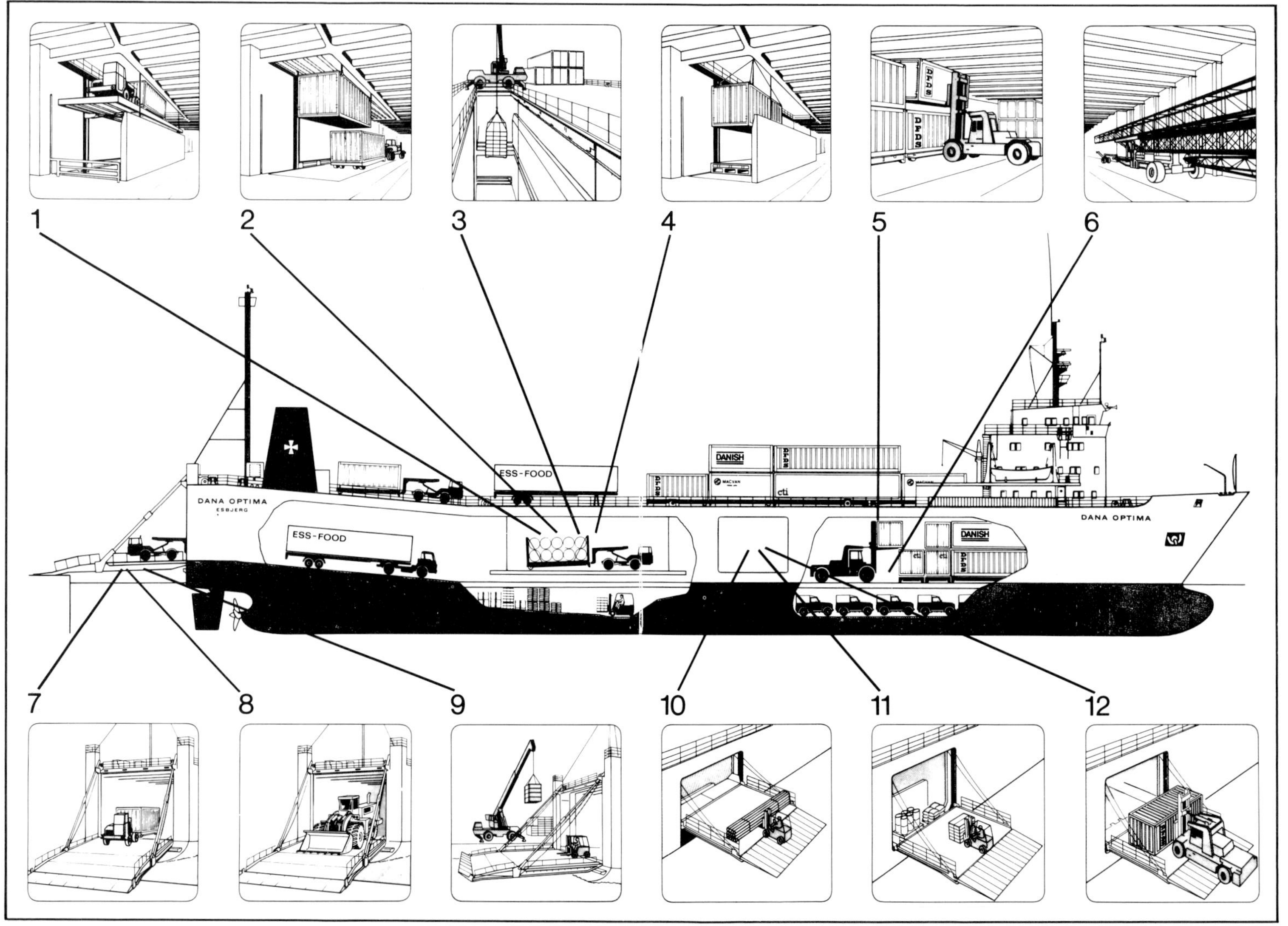

1
2
3
4
5
6
7
8
9
10
11
12
DANA OPTIMA
ESBJERG
ESS-FOOD
ESS-FOOD
DANISH
DANISH
DFDS
MACVAN
cti
DANA OPTIMA

modating some 20 trailers, the *Empire Gaelic* was one of these converted LSTs of the early 1950s. In the late 1950s these were superseded by Transport Ferry Service's ro/ro cargo ships of the *Cedric Ferry* type, providing through-deck stowage for 355 linear metres of cargo on the vehicle deck and 90 linear metres of lift-on units on the weather deck. These were further improved upon, then came a third generation, of the *Tor Gothia* type. These were 18kts vessels with three decks and a carrying capacity of 1,500 linear metres. The lower hold could take both trailers and containers on wheels. The fourth generation ships were exemplified by the two DFDS ships *Dana Futuria* and *Dana Gloria*, with capacities of 402 TEU, and able to discharge full cargoes in six hours. The *Dana Gloria* is designed to transport wheeled freight or containers on slave trailers on the tank top and two trailer decks. The weather deck is above and is served by a 25-ton gantry and movable ramps. Trailers are loaded via two double stern ramps.

When looking at ocean-going ro/ro ships, one landmark in their development was the series of four first generation 16,000 dwt Atlantic Container Line (ACL) ships (1967) which combined a stern entry ro/ro capability with lift-on/lift-off container capacity (569 TEU). The first was the *Atlantic Span*. A second generation of six larger 18,000 dwt ACL ships entered service in 1969-70 and a complete outfit of automated equipment was produced, including flush weather deck hatch covers, stern ramps, side, stern and bulkhead doors and a long hatch cover/ramp. ACL's third generation ro/ro containerships combined flexibility between lo/lo, ro/ro and cars and were 35,433 dwt (36,000 metric tonnes).

A turning point in ro/ro design was Transatlantic Rederi's three Pacific American Direct (PAD) Line ships. The *Perella* (1970) was the first large ro/ro ship to

Leading the new OmniCarrier fleet of the DFDS Nordana Line, which will provide the only ro/ro ships trading between the US Gulf ports and the Mediterranean, is the *Dana America* — a 7,950 dwt vessel featuring a 120-ton capacity derrick for extra heavy cargo. *DFDS*

incorporate an angled stern ramp, designed to be independent of shoreside facilities. Five ro/ro ships based on the earlier PAD vessels were subsequently built in 1972-3. They were 207m long and 22,000 dwt, and had container capacities of about 1,400 TEU, with hold capacities of 52,863cu m. There were four continuous decks below the weather deck, all linked by fixed ramps, including the weather deck. The pinciple was to divide the traffic flow into as many separate driveways as possible as soon as it came on board.

Although ro/ro vessels have been adopted as a solution in many parts of the world, the unique requirements of a continent as large as Australia have tended to accelerate the development and adoption of new approaches by Australian owners, often ahead of larger maritime nations. In the majority of cases Australian owners adopted the use of heavy forklift trucks in contrast to the wheeled trailers or units so popular with European operators.

The first ro/ro vessel in Australia was the *Princess of Tasmania*, built in 1959 for the government-owned Australian National Line (ANL). It was essentially a passenger ferry plying between Tasmania and the mainland. It was joined in 1961 by the *Bass Trader*, a vehicle deck vessel of 1,515 dwt designed exclusively for the carriage of cargo. In August 1962 the first ro/ro service was in augurated between the North and South islands of New Zealand. The vessel, named *Aramoana*, carried 700 passengers, up to 34 rail wagons or 85 motor cars on the vehicle deck, with a further 31 cars on the upper deck.

A regular scheduled service was introduced between the mainland of Sydney and Melbourne and Hobart in the south of Tasmania in 1964, with the first of two sisterships, the *Seaway Queen*, and soon afterwards came the *Seaway King*. Both vessels were 3,105 dwt with a speed of $16\frac{1}{2}$kts. During the 1960s the USS Co began a similar service on the New Zealand coast with

Optima ro/ro vessel showing design characteristics. **1** 55 ton lift; **2** Boye hooks; **3** Mobile crane; **4** Loading on main deck; **5** Double stacking; **6** Roomy main deck; **7, 8, 9** stern ramp (showing various uses); **10, 11, 12**. Wide side door (showing various uses).

The twin-screw *Cicero*, 7,500 tonnes dwt, which was built by Smith's Dock for EWL, Hull.   *Smith's Dock*

two ships both over 2,000 dwt. The *Hawea* began a weekly service between Auckland, Wellington and Dunedin in 1967 and was followed in 1970 by the *Waneka*. In 1966 the USS Co took delivery of the *Wahine*, essentially a passenger ferry with provisions for carrying private automobiles. This, unfortunately, capsized and sank after a short time and her replacement was a similar vessel, the *Rangatira*.

Introduced into Australia at about that time was another passenger ro/ro vessel, the *Empress of Australia*, followed by a third vessel, *Australian Trader* in 1969. Also in 1969, ANL introduced the vehicle deck ship *Australian Enterprise*, which trades between Australia and Japan, plus three Australian-built all-cargo ro/ros to operate between mainland ports. In 1969 and 1970 the *Maheno* and *Marama* were introduced into the trade between the Australian ports of Sydney and Melbourne and the New Zealand ports of Wellington, Auckland and Lyttleton.

The *Iron Monarch* (1973) and *Iron Duke* (1974) represented a new era in ro/ro vessels since they were specifically designed for the carriage of a single type of cargo, namely steel production. The *Iron Monarch* was followed by two vessels, the *Lysaght Enterprise* and *Lysaght Endeavour*, commissioned in 1973 for the ANL and built for the carriage of steel coil but with provision to stack 20ft ISO containers. As a result of increasing ro/ro acceptance by shippers, ANL decided to inaugurate a regular ro/ro service to Japan, of which the *Australian Enterprise* previously mentioned, was the first to be introduced, followed quickly by three sister ships all operated within the Australian Searoad Services. The vessels were of 14,083 dwt, with a service speed of 21kts. These vessels have now been replaced by larger second generation vessels with a deadweight of 23,111 tons and a service speed of 22.75kts.

In America, the *Comet* has already been mentioned as the prototype for ro/ro development and was delivered to the Military Sea Transportation Service (MSTS) in January 1958. In April 1967 a larger and improved version of the *Comet*, the *Sea Lift*, was delivered to MSTS, followed shortly afterwards by the *Admiral William Callaghan* for charter to MSTS. Development of ro/ro shipping in America leant toward trailer carriers (as against the warehouse-type by Europeans), and the commercial version of the *Admiral Wm. Callaghan*, the *Ponce de Leon*, was the first of several trailer vessels built for Transamerican Trailer Transport (TTT).

Ro/ro ships have been built for many parts of the globe and have penetrated many trade routes. For instance, in 1977 deep sea ro/ro operators Seaspeed Services inaugurated a regular service from Japan and North America to the Middle East. The service incorporated a 'feeder' service to shallow draught ports. In 1979 the DFDS Norada Line added four new ro/ro ships to its fleet. Designed for great versatility, the ships were to operate between the US Gulf and the Mediterranean, the first to go into service being the *Dana America*. These ships were believed to be the first ro/ro vessels on the route at the time. That same year the naming of the 7,200 dwt ro/ro freighter marked the inauguration of the 'Polanglia' service between the UK and Poland.

Ro/ro ships have grown considerably over the years, one of the largest in the world is the *Seaspeed Arabia*, while Italy has contributed to the world's growing fleet of jumbo ro/ros with the building in 1980 of two 28,500 dwt third generation ro/ro ships, the *Andrea Marzario* and the *Comadante Revello* at Italcantieri's Monfalcone yard. The vessels were designed on the 'open ship' principle and equipped with particularly large stern ramps. Delivered to Andrea Merzario SpA of Milan in 1981, the vessels represented a further step in the process of steamlining the loading of ro/ro cargoes while also reducing the need for port facilities of any kind, except for a flat area of wharf on which to park a stern ramp.

A number of innovations have occurred in ro/ro

The *Lurline*, 13,860 dwt, built by Sun for the Matson Line.
Sun Shipbuilding

design and construction in recent years. For example, a unique heavy lift ro/ro ship, *Starman*, was launched in 1974, being strengthened to take loads of up to 1,000 tons. A novel way to build ro/ro vessels was demonstrated by the Navire yard in Finland with its floating construction of the 4,550 dwt ship *Bia* in 1976. That same year two triple-decked articulated tug-barge ro/ro vessels were ordered in the USA, employing the ARTUBAR system developed by E. H. Fletcher, while the deep-sea ro/ro vessel *Boogabilla*, completed in 1978, included among its revolutionary features a large-bore slow speed diesel engine, three parallel trafficways and a jumbo angled stern ramp.

Ramps have been of considerable interest to designers of ro/ros. In 1975 the lead ro/ro ship of a series of six for the USSR, the *Akademic Tupolev*, was completed and of special interest in its design was the system of access ramps, including a quarter ramp in three sections and a large multi-purpose internal ramp, adjustable for loading on four different decks. In 1977 the *Rabenfels*, one of two sister ro/ro ships was fitted with the first ever stern slewing ramps for such vessels. The ramps were designed by Navire Cargo Gear International A/B and revolved on a friction free surface through a turning radius of 12.5m. That same year two similar ships, the *Reichenfels* and *Rheinfels*, were fitted with MacGregor stern slewing ramps, which comprise three main sections: the folding ramp itself, 35m long when fully extended, a turntable and two driving winches. Yet another Navire angled ramp was fitted in 1979 to the first of five 6,800 dwt ro/ro ships, the *Hua Yuan Kou*.

Looking at some recent ro/ro constructions, the twin-screw ro/ro vessels *Cicero* and *Cavallo*, 7,500 tonnes dwt, were built by Smith's Dock for EWL, Hull. A very new building is represented by the first of a new generation of Finnish ro/ros which was launched in 1982 at the Rauma-Repola Yard, Rauma, Finland for service between Finland and the UK's east coast ports, this 9,000grt vessel has its upper deck mainly for lorry traffic. The deck is enclosed to give weather protection such as is found on the *Baltic Eagle*, but with the idea extended to where the foredeck is also decked over to prevent ice forming on the mooring gear.

Designers thoughts have turned toward gas turbines as a means of powering ro/ro vessels. Soviet designers have been looking at gas turbine applications since the building of the *Parizsakaya Kommuna* in the 1960s, the first ever gas turbine-powered cargo vessel. The gas turbine-powered ro/ro ship *Kapitan Smirnov* was built for the USSR and delivered in 1980. This vessel was the first of two 20,000dwt ro/ro's with a speed of 25kts, and utilises exhaust gas from two reversing gas turbines to generate sufficient steam to power supplementary steam turbines. Before this, the *Iron Monarch* mentioned previously, was one of the first commercial vessels installed with a heavy duty gas turbine, while the Australian-built 14,550dwt Ro/ro ship *Rotorua*, delivered in 1977, had gas turbine power for its main machinery.

Multi-purpose ships are becoming increasingly attractive, and the Bo-RO project has already been mentioned in the Bulk Carrier chapter. An offshoot of the ro/ro principle is the combination ro/ro and container carrier, which in some people's opinion is the ideal answer for certain trades and routes. Some of the design parameters to consider in the selection of such vessels is that they are basically 'horizontally wide open' ships with no transverse obstruction such as bulkheads in the main cargo spaces. A stern ramp seems a necessity and for larger vessels, a slewing ramp that can be operated in at least three directions (port, starboard and aft) appears desirable. One example of such a vessel is the *Hellenic Explorer* (1978), owned by Hellenic Lines Ltd. Another vessel, this time built in the USA is the *John B. Waterman*, constructed in 1982, the first of a class of three combined ro/ro and container ships built by Sun Ship Inc for the Waterman Steamship Corp, and the largest self-loading ro/ro yet built in that country.

General Cargo Ships

For the purposes of this chapter the general cargo ship will cover a miscellaneous variety of vessels, including dry cargo ships, refrigerated vessels, coasters and those cargo vessels that may broadly be categorised as other than ro/ro or container ships.

Beginning first with a very general description of a cargo vessel, it is typically a flat-bottomed steel structure divided by watertight transverse bulkheads into compartments which form the holds and machinery space. The holds may also be divided by one or two decks with hatchways giving access to the lower spaces. The vessel will usually have a double bottom consisting of an inner and outer skin, with tanks between for oil fuel and water ballast. Lifting arrangements such as derricks and winches are incorporated in the design, and modern vessels are equipped with labour-saving steel-hinged hatch covers.

Another type of cargo vessel is the cargo liner, which runs to a fixed timetable between two or more ports. The profile of these vessels varies considerably but a compact superstructure is common, while the modern trend is to locate engines aft. The cargo liner's speed may be as high as 19-20kts or more. A recent such vessel of this type is the 22,000 dwt *Menalaus*, first of four to be built for the Barbar Line in 1977, for service between Asia and American ports.

The tramp ship, which indicates a type of employment rather than a vessel type, can be a general cargo ship or bulk carrier, and plays a nomadic role in sea trade. It will deliver or collect cargo to or from any port in any area, according to the demands of trade.

The refrigerated cargo ship — of which more will be said later — is designed for the carriage of fruit, meat or other perishable cargoes. Insulation of the compartments may be by cork, mineral wool, or glass wool. The refrigerated fruit ship is usually of medium size and is capable of higher speeds than the cargo ship of comparable dimensions. The refrigerated meat ship is generally much larger than the fruit ship and is employed on longer voyages.

There is then the coaster and short-sea trader, which operates in coastal waters on short-sea routes and may be employed as a collier. Up to about 70m in length, these vessels usually have machinery aft, and some have raised quarter decks. Derricks and deck machinery are fitted on deck to handle the variety of cargoes that such vessels carry.

The Japanese in the 1950s built cargo liners of 11-12,000 dwt, powered with diesel engines and having a service speed of 17-18kts. The ships were known as 'flush-deckers with forecastle', having machinery amidships. There were three holds forward, the same aft. Later on the size of these vessels increased.

Around 1957 the 'Mariner' class of American liners made its debut on the New York-Japan route, and all the while service speeds were being increased. This was made possible by high supercharging for diesel engines and the design of better hull forms. Another innovation in the design of cargo ships was the introduction of greater automation, which extended to mooring operations and the programmed control of propulsive machinery. This drastically reduced the ship's complement, sometimes by as much as half, thus providing greater economy in operating costs.

The 1960s saw even greater increase in speeds, in conjunction with lower powers. The Japanese were the main instigators of this, starting with *Yamashiro Mara* in 1963, which attained a speed of 19.5kts with only 13,000bhp. This vessel was also an early example of a ship having a bulbous bow. From then on speed continued to rise until the 20kts standard was reached, and eventually ships were achieving 25kts.

Tramping has been on the decline for several years, having lost a large part of its traffic in minerals. But in the sphere of basic agricultural products such as cereals and oilseeds the tramp steamer still holds its own. This is because of factors such as variable harvests, weather conditions and so on, by which these products may be affected. In these unstable conditions the tramp ship supplies the necessary tonnage at short notice, and therefore needs to be equipped for the transportation of bulk cargoes. Shifting boards, feeders and other equipment that controls the shifting and compacting of cargo have undergone development in the past 20 years. For the latest designs — in accordance with present-day IMO requirements — such equipment is no longer used due to a number of factors, involving modified regulations, stability, etc.

The tramp ship also deals in manufactured goods insofar where this is also irregular, while on occasion coming to the aid of regular lines when there are excess cargoes. In summary, the tramp ship must be able to handle a number of cargoes, must be able to enter average sized ports, and must be able to accomplish long trips in ballast.

Refrigerated ships may be considered as a specialised form of cargo ship and nowadays many types of cargo are carried under refrigeration, such as meat, bananas, citrus fruit, shellfish, etc. Each commodity is kept at a temperature suitable to it, and there are two ways by which the air in a refrigerated space is cooled. The first, and older, system is the grid system, which cools the air via a grid of cold pipes covering the sides and ceiling of the compartment. These pipes absorb the heat from the air. Newer installations adopt the forced draught system where the air from the cargo holds is passed by fans over a bank of refrigerated pipes then distributed through a ducting system.

Dr John Gorrie, an American, introduced his cold air machine in 1849, then in the early part of this century refrigeration development was rapid. From about 1920 onwards little change occurred in the methods of carriage of refrigerated cargoes, except that Freon type gases replaced carbon dioxide as the refrigerant. In the 1950s containerisation was introduced, and refrigerated containers came on the scene.

Two basic types of containers are used for refrigerated cargoes, and both are based on the 20ft ISO module. The first type — a quite simple unit — is used on refrigerated container vessels and has two ventilating ports situated at the opposite ends to the doors. These ports are aligned with the vessel's ducting system, which operates in a similar manner to the forced draught system. The second type — a much more expensive and sophisticated module — is fitted with its own refrigerating machinery and can be carried on any ship, usually on those where there is a smaller flow of refrigerated cargo, thus not requiring a specialised vessel.

An interesting postwar design of vessel is the open-hatch ship, which was created in the design offices of Philip F. Spalding of Seattle, consulting ship designer,

Loading cargo ships hasn't changed a great deal in postwar years. Here two cargoes for Singapore are loaded on to Ben Line ships: (*left*) Morrises are lifted on the *Bencleuch* in the early postwar years; (*right*) Caterpillar tractors on to *Benrinnes* in the 1970s. *Ben Line*

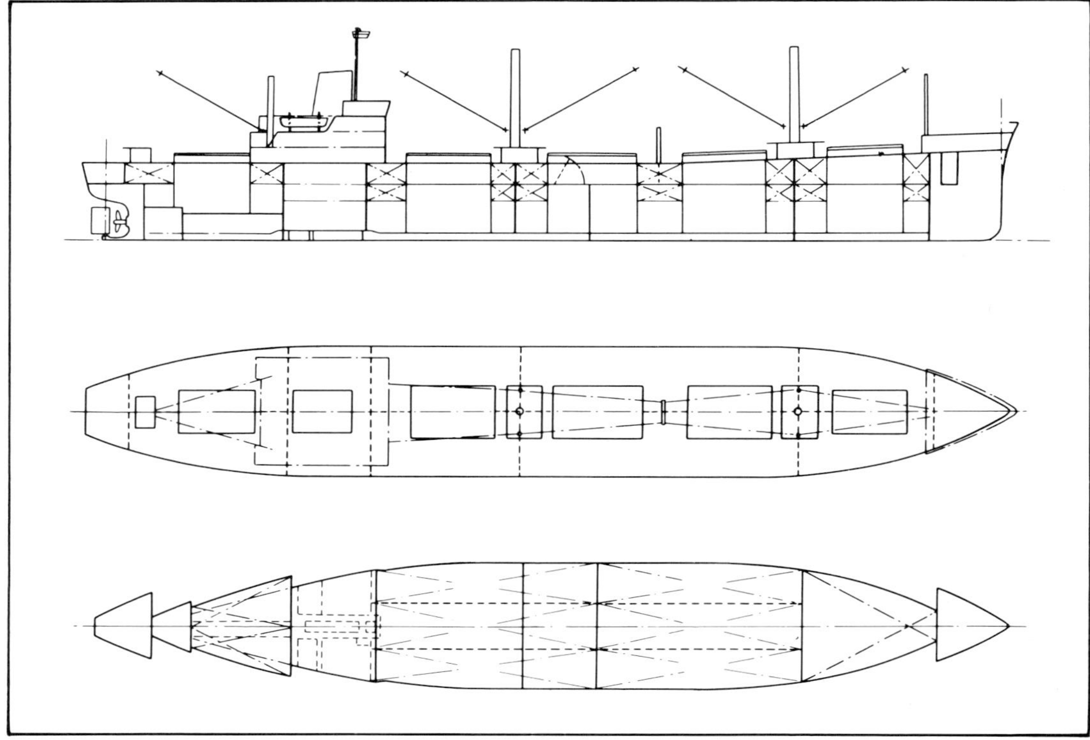

Diagram of the Austin & Pickersgill SD14.

in 1960. This innovative vessel was developed for the newsprint trade, with the major aim being to reduce cargo handling costs. The cargo holds can be described as giant open topped boxes, completely smooth-sided and with all internal bulkheads eliminated. Rolls of newsprint are stacked one on top of the other to the full depth of hold. This is done by using rolling gantry cranes lifting eight rolls at a time by means of a spreader frame suspended from the crane lifting wires. The hatches are covered by hydraulically-powered hinge-up folding hatch covers. The first ship of this type was launched in 1962 and christened *MV Bessegen.*

Yet another interesting type of cargo vessel — if it can be classified purely as such — is the multi-purpose ship. A number of standard ships have been designed for general cargo duties, but also able to be modified for multi-purpose and bulk cargoes. Among these are Austin & Pickersgill's popular SD14 which is now in its fourth series. This series-built 15,000 dwt general cargo vessel is suitable for worldwide trading, with scantlings suitable for it to sail fully loaded with the deep tank empty. Its 144m long hull is designed to give efficient performance in all conditions of loading, while also providing good basic stability. A&P concentrated on the building of standard ships quite a while ago and since the completion of the first three SD14s in 1968 over 200 have been ordered from A&P and its licencees. The company also have the compact SD9 cargo vessel and the SD18 cargo ship, as well as the B30 and B35 bulk carriers.

IHI have built many cargo ships for specific purposes, such as the chip carrier, *Eiyoh Maru,* 36,182grt, and the lumber carrier *Meiten Maru,* 11,912grt. But the company has also produced the well known F-series standardised multi-purpose cargo ships which are offered in five basic types: Freedom, Freedom Mark-II, Fortune-32, Future-45 and Future-60. This standardisation has brought about many advantages in costs and operation, such as low ship prices, reduced fuel consumption and simplified chartering and documentation routines through rationalised designs and standardised specifications. One Freedom Mark-II ship is the *Efdim Hope,* 17,181 dwt. A Friendship type vessel is the *Anangel Fidelity,* 23,568 dwt, while a Fortune ship is the *Chimo,* 22,536 dwt.

Multi-purpose ships known as Liberty replacements, such as those mentioned above, first appeared in 1967/8 and earned reputations for economy and versatility. These 'tweendeck' ships are suited to both general and bulk cargoes such as grain, particularly for trading to relatively shallow draught ports.

Considering some recent building of cargo vessels, the 20,000 dwt *Capitan Smirnov* made its maiden voyage in 1979 and was the USSR's fastest merchant vessel at the time. In that same year the first of a new 'winter' class of reefer (refrigerated cargo) ships, the *Winter Moon,* came into service. Its concept was based on palletised unit handling but it can also accommodate break bulk and conventional cargoes, as well as cars and has a capacity for 240 TEU. Earlier in 1975 the specialised reefer ship *Almeda Star* was launched.

Two typical early postwar cargo ships: (*above*) the three-island *Ceres* of 1944; and (*right*) *City of Port Elizabeth* a cargo/passenger ship of 1952. *Real Photos*

The *Al Muharraq* (*below*), one of 19 'Kuwait' class ships built by Govan Shipbuilders, setting off down the Clyde. *Govan*

The 9,750 dwt refrigerated/dry cargo vessel *Geestbay* built by Smith's Dock in 1980. She can take 12 passengers and a load of bananas from Windward Island to Barry.   *Smith's Dock*

This vessel was the last of a series of five 11,000 dwt vessels for the Blue Star Line. In 1977 the cargo liner *Menalaus*, previously mentioned, was the first of four such vessels to join the Barbar Line. Yet another cargo liner, the *Salta*, was launched in 1976 and was the first of a series of three for Lineas Maritimas Argentinas. These ships were based on the SD14 design.

To conclude this section on general cargo ships, and before finally discussing the coaster, a look is taken at one major UK shipping company of long standing, who has run general cargo ships and other types for well over 100 years. The company is the Ben Line and the beginnings may be traced to James Thomson, an Edinburgh builder with a substantial interest in Italian marble, whose two sons set up their own account as shipbrokers in 1825. The maritime interests of A. and W. Thomson grew rapidly as the building trade declined, and a large part of this was due to its financial connections with two Alloa families, Thomsons and Mitchells. The company gravitated from sail to steam and its first steamship was the *Benledi*. The prefix 'Ben' is an English approximation of the Gaelic word for

mountain and to this day is ubiquitous in the company's naming of its fleet, the first such ship being the *Bencleuch* in 1853. Today, the company is involved in many aspects of marine transport, including container ships, oil tankers and bulk carriers, and is also involved in the offshore side, and a number of present and past Ben Line cargo vessels are illustrated in this chapter.

The coaster or short-sea trader is an all-purpose cargo ship that plies the coast or short stretches of water. Such vessels are often seen in small or large ports, or in up-river quays. Some coasters run to a regular timetable and may be classed as specialised 'liners', while many other coasters are employed as colliers on either regular coastal, or irregular short-sea routes. The types serving the regular routes have no cargo gear but rely on port handling facilities and equipment to load and discharge.

The typical coaster may be up to 70m in length, having a profile somewhat like that of a miniature cargo ship, and with a gross tonnage under 2,000. Early coasters had raised quarter-decks that extended well forward — almost to amidships or beyond to give a better trim when loaded — but modern vessels have them much shorter or a poop only. Invariably the machinery is well aft so that valuable space is not taken up by a shaft tunnel. Powerful derricks and cranes are usually installed to enable the handling of a variety of cargoes in ports lacking adequate handling facilities. To protect the vessel from damage a rubbing strake is

The large Russian merchant fleet of the Baltic Shipping Co has a number of dry cargo vessels — for example the 12,295 dwt *Vyborg*. *Baltic Shipping Ço*

A selection of Ben Line vessels showing the changes to cargo ships over the years: (*above*) *Bennevis* which saw service between 1928 and 1941; (*right*) *Benarty* at Tarying Proik dock, Indonesia; and (*below*) *Benledi* and *Benreoch* in London Docks.
Ben Line (two), Skyfotos

The Kawasaki-built cargo liner *Hôegh Mallard. Kawasaki*

fitted round the hull, while other features may include a soft-nosed stem and flat bottom to unload when grounded.

Design developments in coasters since World War 2 have included the 'tweendeck' designs, open and closed shelterdeckers and the introduction of double skins in certain hull constructions. Another development has been the design of low draught coasters. The decline of coal as a major fuel in power stations due to the increased use of oil, has led to a drastic reduction in the number of colliers, but the last two decades or so has also seen the introduction of many specialised coasters, and those that can carry containers, palletised units or even incorporate ro/ro facilities. Some are even designed as mini-reefers. In fact, multi-purpose coasters have evolved to exploit the short sea trade, while the variety of cargoes has expanded to include many break-bulk, homogeneous and even liquid and gas cargoes.

One type of coastal vessel that has become prominent in European waters since 1945 is the Dutch coaster. Developed in Holland for operating in very shallow estuaries, rivers and canals, it has a very shallow draught, engines and accommodation aft, a large hold, electric cargo machinery and a strong hull to enable it to lie well on the ground at low water. The Dutch coaster became an influential force in British home trade soon after World War 1. Of just under 500 tons, this type of vessel is unique in the fact that the captain owns the vessel while his family contribute to the crew, although this type of familial structure is now being displaced in favour of corporate-owned vessels of much larger deadweight.

The expansion of British and Continental waterways in recent years has led to an increase in the coaster trade, which has also resulted in the increased use of low air draught coasters which can deliver goods direct from British ports to Continental destinations well inland. Earlier versions of this type of vessel were in the 400-600 dwt range.

Looking at some of the various coasters built in recent years, the coaster *Commodity* was launched in July 1975, designed for the carriage of general cargo on short-sea routes. The *Lady Sandra*, a 380 dwt coaster built by James W. Cook & Co (Wivenhoe) Ltd, was designed for near Continental and home trading requirements, with special consideration being given to

United Enterprise is a 'SD14' type vessel built by Govan Shipbuilders and completed in 1982. *AirFotos*

An IHI 'Friendship Mk II' ship, the 17,181 dwt *Efdim Hope*.
IHI

good helm characteristics when operating in confined
waterways on the Continent and inland home ports. A
short-sea cargo vessel is the 1,350 dwt *Bongo*,
specialising in Baltic and North Sea trades and frequently penetrating deep into the canal and river
systems of Europe.

One vessel designed to carry a variety of cargoes is
the 2,450 dwt *Ingar*, which specialises mainly in the
shipment of paper, wood pulp, long items such as
piping, and grain, coal and bulk salt. A coastal vessel
that incorporates ro/ro facilities is the 1,370 dwt *Saint
Brandan*, yet another James Cook vessel and a
development of the company's Colne class, which
covers a deadweight range of 300-1,800 dwt. The
vessel has a bow ramp for ro/ro cargohandling and can
carry loads of up to approximately 300 tons on the
hatch. The foremast is of goalpost design to allow large
wheeled loads to pass through, while the hull is suitable for loading aground and has all-flat bottom plates
so that bottom damage is less costly to repair.

A closed/open shelterdeck type is represented by the

A typical collier, the *Accum* of 1950.   *Real Photos*

The *Andalucia Star* is a typical refrigerated ship, built for the Blue Star Line.   *Skyfotos*

Dutch built *Ailda Smits*, the first in a series of six. In the open mode the vessel's gross tonnage remains under 1,600, while as a closed ship the gross tonnage is well under 4,000. The 3,920 dwt *M. V. Emerald* is the second of two identical shelterdeck bulk carriers from the Cleland shipyard, which is included among the Small Ship Group of British Shipbuilders. The vessel is double-skinned in way of the cargo holds, leaving two clear holds and tweendecks. It is capable of carrying all types of bulk and timber cargoes and is arranged for container carrying in the holds and one tier on the cargo hatches.

Clelands also designed and built a new breed of low air-draught coasters in 1978, the 1,400 dwt *Militance* being the first. One special feature of the design was the choice of a Schilling rudder for high manoeuvrability.

The coastal vessel *Fastnet* of 1965.   *Real Photos*

11

Heavy Lift Ships

Heavy lift ships are difficult to categorise within a particular type, but because heavy lift cargo is carried either by liner-type or general cargo vessels with a heavy lift capability, or by heavy lift ships which provide a specialised heavy lift service in the so-called 'tramping' trade, these vessels seem to fit more appropriately within this chapter, although they could obviously warrant a chapter of their own.

Among the first to tackle the problem of heavy lift transportation successfully was the Norwegian Christen Smith, born in 1883, who had a significant influence on the heavy lift scene between the wars. But the greatest developments in heavy lift transportation over water has occurred during postwar years. It has become one of the most expanding areas of marine transportation. Immediately after World War 2 the Ben Line became involved in heavy lift shipments and the German fleet ships built during the early postwar years were equipped with heavy lift gear which had been developed 23 years earlier. The essential feature of a 1950-type handling gear was the 25-ton boom operating in one direction only and requiring a total of 10 men and a supervisor to operate. In 1954 a novel type heavy lift handling gear was supplied and installed by the shipyard Stülcken & Sohn, Hamburg, on the *Lichtenfels*. Modern heavy lift gears can now lift far greater loads than those early postwar efforts, and with fewer men. In fact, there are over 2,000 ships in the world fleet with lifting capabilties ranging from 50 to 1,000 tons — for example Kawasaki's 600-ton heavy cargo derrick — although it must be said that a large number of these have a lifting capability below 100 tons.

The present growth in heavy lift transportation is due to the increase in cargoes of high value and increased weight and dimensions, brought about by worldwide industrialisation coupled with plant expansion and modernisation. Designers and builders have responded to the situation by introducing modern specialised heavy lift ships of various types, capable of worldwide transportation with unit weights of up to 1,000 tons. Heavy lift cargoes include such main items as electrical power equipment, nuclear power reactors, engines and machinery of various types, as well as construction and military equipment, locomotives, etc.

There are a variety of heavy lift vessels which can be categorised under certain basic concepts. The first and most widely-known and applied concept is lift-on/lift-off (lo/lo), which is used by about all liner-type heavy lift ships such as general cargo vessels with heavy lift capabilities, as well as typical barge-carrying vessels. For liner-type heavy lift general cargo vessels sets of heavy lift derricks of various designs are fitted to serve the hatches. The vessels' range of sizes of approximately 10,000-22,000 dwt make them unsuitable for shallow water ports. Specialised heavy lift vessels normally range in size from 1,000-7,000 dwt, with lifting capacities of up to 800 tons. Their cargo is usually handled by two sets of lifting gear of various designs. The increasing demands in heavy lift transportation have also led to the use of the Catamaran system, which basically consists of the temporary joining together of two vessels.

Another concept uses the pure ro/ro principle, but such heavy lift vessels, which have no other means of cargo transfer, are in the minority. Their sizes range from about 1,500 to a maximum of 5,000 dwt, and they are generally fitted with either stern or bow ramps, being able to transfer loads of about 1,000 tons. A drive-through capability is provided for by designing the superstructure in a 'bridge-type' manner. Because this type of vessel has no other means of cargo transfer than ro/ro, auxiliary transfer equipment such as crawlers, wheeled transport, etc, is usually required.

The 650-ton heavy derrick *Malacca Maru*. *Kawasaki*

Diagram of heavy lift slewing derrick.

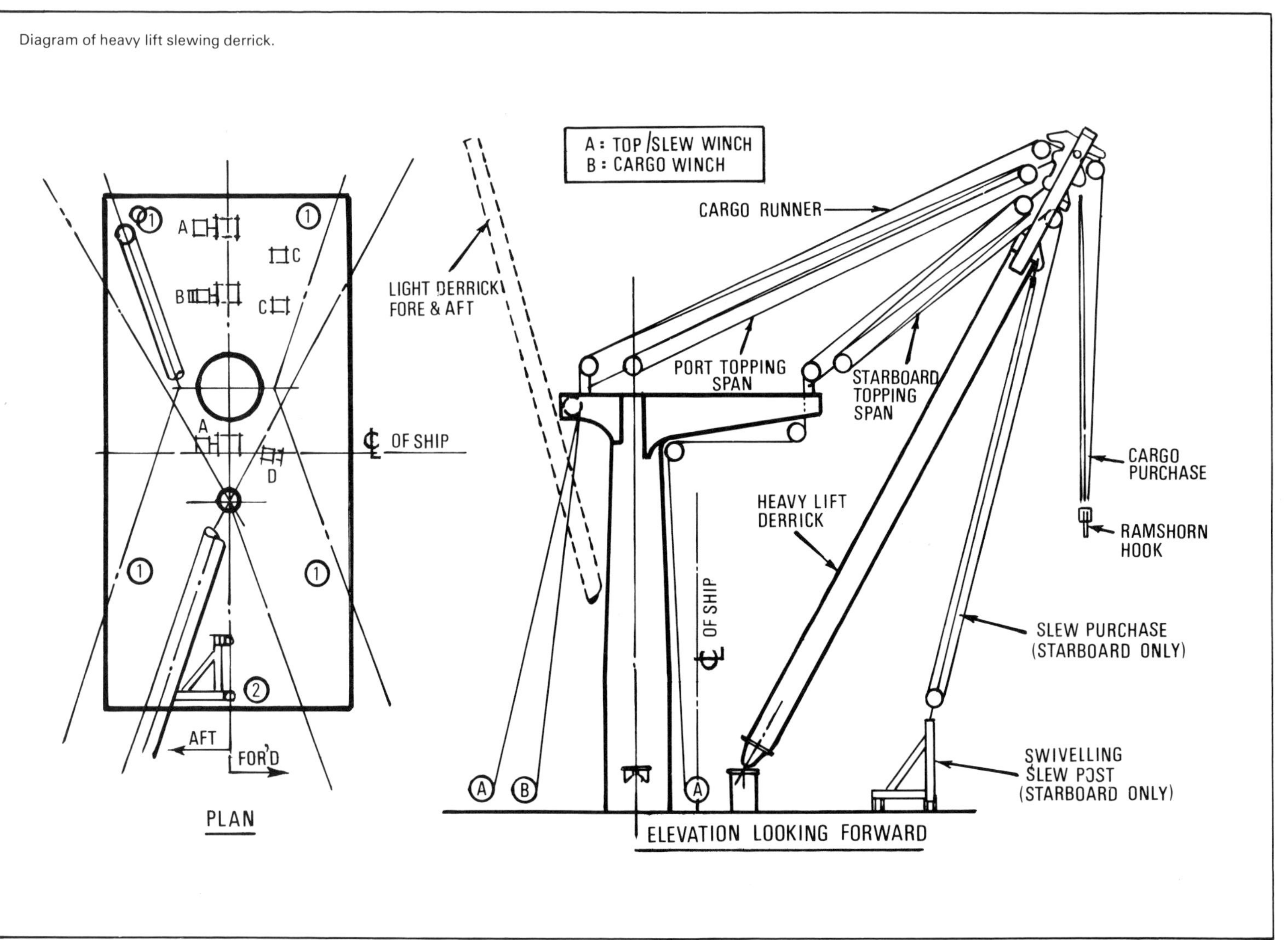

A third concept combines both the lo/lo and ro/ro principles and is known — logically enough! — as lo/lo-ro/ro. Such vessels are basically lift-on/lift-off ships with the added capability of transferring cargo by ro/ro methods. They usually range in size from about 1,200-6,000 dwt and have bow ramps with associated stern ramps to provide the ro/ro feature. To also allow uninterupted ro/ro through capability the heavy lift gear is normally fitted off the centreline of ship, and in many instances completely outboard. Specialised auxiliary transport similar to the ro/ro only heavy lift ships is employed. The lo/lo capability of such ships is up to 800 tons, while the ro/ro and through capability is up to 1,000 tons. To take advantage of the possible ro/ro demands, the vessels are normally of shallow draught design to permit loading or discharge of cargo directly ashore.

One other concept that comes under the heavy lift category is the float-on/float-off (flo/flo) concept, which has been in existence for many years. Typical vessels of this type are also referred to as self-propelled drydocks. The military version is the LSD type vessel, while commercial types carry barges, tugs, dredgers and other floating vessels. The floating cargo enters the ship's submerged well at the stern and when the well is pumped dry it rests on the tank top of the ship, to be more firmly secured later. A stern gate completely seals the well from the outside sea. Such vessels are mainly designed to transport floating cargoes of up to 12,500 tons. There is also the semi-submersible vessel, which utilises her floating feature to receive floating cargoes either sideways, by submerging the vessel in the horizontal position, or over the bow by grounding the fore part. Flo/Flo vessels can also be capable of receiving ro/ro cargoes, or be fitted with the additional capability of lo/lo. It may be mentioned that barge-type carriers have already been discussed in greater deal within the appropriate chapter.

Another concept is the slide-on/slide-off one, which is used for relatively short cargo movements, although some vessels use this principle for main cargo transfer. One vessel using this principle is equipped with a hydraulically-operated lift platform for raising and lowering the cargo between the hold and the weather deck, then retractable transfer slide tracks which extend over the vessel's side to the lift platform, are provided for moving the cargo from the shoreside to the lift platform.

Finally, one can classify floating cranes as a type that comes under the heavy lift label. These giant structures perform a number of useful heavy lift tasks, including offshore work. They can be jack-ups, semi-submerged, pontoon-mounted or of other types and can reach capacities up to 3,000 tonnes or even more. One such floating crane is the self-propelled *Binhai 108* built by IHI and with a deadweight tonnage of 4,876 tonnes and capacity 800 tonnes, completed in 1979. An even more powerful IHI floating crane is the non-propelled *Musashi*, with a hoisting capacity of 3,000 tonnes.

Of the various types of heavy lift gear only three are extensively fitted on typical modern heavy lift ships. These are non-rotating derricks, rotating derricks and gantry cranes. There is also the highly flexible revolving crane, capable of lifting up to 2,500 tons, which is mainly used for crane ships in the offshore industry.

An extremely common non-rotating derrick is the Stülcken derrick, previously mentioned. Between 1953 and 1978 over 500 such derricks had been fitted on approximately 460 ships. The first designs had inclined posts in a V-arrangement, and were fitted on their upper portions with rotary topping lift attachments, thus eliminating complex stay and supporting systems. Between the two V-posts was a heavy lift boom on a centre bearing. This system, with slight modifications, is still used today, while the original maximum lifting capacity of 125 tons has now risen to 350 tons and even more.

Rotating derricks have a single tower kingpost of about 4-5m diameter at base with a double-legged boom attached at bottom, which is able to rotate by means of slewing winches. They are capable of 360° rotation and 200-700-ton range for lifting capacity. Gantry cranes for shipboard heavy lift operations are of the travelling type, carrying their load between the lengths of the hold or well. Their lifting capacity range from 250-500 tons.

The 800-tonne self-propelled floating crane *Binhai 108*, built by IHI and completed in 1979. *IHI*

12

Passenger and Cruise Liners

The passenger liner, which though primarily designed for the carriage of passengers, will generally also carry a small amount of cargo. Size and silhouette vary considerably and the outline may be broken by deckhouses and derricks. Early passenger liners did not have the tiers of superstructures now associated with modern vessels, whose aerodynamic lines are more accentuated than their forebears. They also had a narrower beam in association with their length.

The heyday of the luxury passenger liner was between the wars but the first ships specially constructed to carry passengers across the Atlantic were British and American, beginning with the *Great Britain* and *Great Eastern*. The latter was half a century ahead of its time and was not surpassed in size until 49 years later, in 1907, when the *Mauretania* was launched. The *Mauretania* was the sister ship of the *Lusitania*, sunk by a German submarine in 1915, and held the Blue Riband for 22 years. The tragic sinking of the *Titanic* on her maiden voyage led to greater safety standards being set, while other names to conjure up during this period were the French liners *Paris* and *Normandie*, and the Dutch liner *Bloemfontein*. But the most famous of all were the *Queen Mary* and *Queen Elizabeth*, which placed Britain at the head of the world's luxury liners. These floating hotels were the largest, fastest and most luxurious of the passenger giants and regularly crossed the Atlantic in four days.

It was in 1957 that the number of passengers travelling by air first exceeded those travelling by sea. This marked what seemed to be the end of the liner as a regular means of sea transportation between continents and countries; nevertheless the postwar years saw a number of fine passsenger vessels built to serve various routes like — to name a few: the *Edinburgh Castle* of

28,629 grt which was built in 1948 for the Union Castle Line, had a speed of 22kts and carried 705 passengers; the *Orcades* (also of 1948) was built for the Orient Line and converted in 1964 to a 'one class' vessel for 1,635 passengers; and the *Arcadia* and *Iberia*, built in 1954 for the P&O Line with a gross tonnage of 29,614 and a speed of 24.9kts. The latter had accommodation for 1,407 passengers.

The Southern Cross, 19,313grt, was built in 1955 and carried 1,160 passengers at a speed of 20kts. This liner was distinguished by the fact that it was the first passenger liner to have machinery — and therefore funnels — aft. The 1960s saw an increase in gross tonnage. The Italian vessel *Leonardo da Vinci*, built in 1960, had a gross tonnage of 33,340. It carried 1,326 passengers and had a speed of 25kts. *The Canberra*, built in 1961, had a gross tonnage of 43,975 and carried 2,250 passengers at a speed of 27½kts. She has since proved of value as a troopship during the Falklands conflict. The *Empress of Canada*, built in 1961, was 25,780grt and carried 1,048 passengers at a speed of 21kts. Lastly, the Italian vessel *Eugino C*, built in 1966, had a gross tonnage of 30,567 and a passenger capacity of 1,600 with a speed of 27kts.

Three passenger liners of maritime interest and importance in this postwar era are the *United States, France*, and *Queen Elizabeth II*. The first was a Blue Riband holder, the second was the world's longest passenger liner, eventually to be converted into a cruise liner, and the third was Britain's attempt to revive some of its past luxury liner glories.

Dealing with the *France* first; she sailed on her maiden voyage in 1962 and made 400 Atlantic voyages and 93 cruises but was eventually defeated by the high cost of fuel. With a gross tonnage of 66,348, her length of 1,035ft made her the longest passenger ship ever. In 1974 she was laid up in Le Havre then in 1979 was bought by Knut Utstein Kloster who foresaw

The 1957 Blue Star cargo passenger ship *Queensland Star*.
Real Photos

The *Queen Elizabeth* which led the field in luxury sea travel before World War 2.   *Real Photos*

The *Iberia* of 1954.   *Real Photos*

a future for her as flagship of North Carribean Lines. The conversion work added 3,030grt, and with accommodation extended and modernised, she is able to carry 2,000 passengers and more than 700 crew. Renamed the *Norway*, she became the world's largest cruise liner and now has a maximum speed of 21kts and service speed of 16-18kts, as opposed to the *France's* 30kts. Another interesting feature is the grouping of variable pitch side thrusters in order to eliminate the use of tugs, while the original quadruple shafts were reduced to two to obtain a reduction in speed.

The *United States* (1952) was 900ft long and had a gross tonnage of 50,924, carrying 2,008 passengers at a service speed of 28kts. On her maiden voyage she attained a speed of 35.59kts, thus winning the Blue Riband previously held by the *Queen Mary* with 31.69kts. She was bought by United States Cruises in 1979 after being laid up for 12 years, and the intention is to place her in the US West Coast-Hawaii service, although there are some legal wrangles to overcome.

The *Queen Elizabeth II*, built to try and recapture some of the glory of the past two queens, was completed in 1969 for Cunard but was smaller than her two antecedents, being 962ft in length. She carried 2,025 passengers at a speed of $28\frac{1}{2}$kts and one distinctive feature is the unusual funnel which is designed to throw soot and gases well clear of the decks. Initially, she was intended for service on the Southampton-New York route in season, and does 12 trips each way every year. She was also designed to utilise the Panama Canal for cruising in the winter months. Since her completion she has had a new storey added, plus minor modifications elsewhere, and her gross tonnage is now 67,000 tons. During the Falklands conflict she was conscripted into military service as a troopship and formed a valuable part of the task force that was despatched to the Atlantic. On her return she was restored to her original luxury state, and other passenger amenities are also added, together with a 'new look' appearance of all-white.

The *Southern Cross* of 1955 was the first passenger liner to have its machinery — and, therefore, funnel — aft. *Real Photos*

France (1961) later modified to become the largest cruise liner in the world as the *Norway*.   *Real Photos*

Despite such fine vessels as mentioned above, the days of the regular liner service were numbered. A chapter of marine history closed when the *Windsor Castle*, built in 1960, completed her last voyage on the South Africa passenger mail service in 1977, to be then sold to Greek owners. Following this, the *Dwarka* — the last British registered liner — terminated its sea time in 1982. Nevertheless, there was to be a new lease of life for passenger liners. A welcome expansion in the holiday market, together with an increase in prosperity, happened in the sixties and suddenly holiday cruises were big business, enabling support to the failing liner service. Cruising has been a form of vacationing since the 1840s and had a brief period of glory in the early 1930s. The postwar expansion in this field rejuvenated what seemed an almost defunct side of marine transportation. The main initiative came from Norway and most of the ships were built to carry 600/700 passengers at a speed of 18-19kts. They were to form the first generation of a new type. The market peaked in 1979 and orders for a new generation of ships were placed. The vessels now being built will carry 1,200/1,400 passengers at speeds of 20-22kts, with a gross tonnage of around 35,000 tons.

The growth of cruising saw 25 new vessels built between 1970 and 1975, although there was a setback in the late 1970s due to the oil crisis and subsequent rapid inflation of operating costs. By 1982 there was a dramatic upturn with nine new vessels under construction and another eight undergoing major reconstruction. In all, over 52 cruise lines were operating more than 150 vessels serving the main cruise areas of the world.

The trend in cruise ships at the beginning was to build class ships, ie a series of identical vessels for the same owner. Class building became prolific in the 1970s, although several series were built in the 1960s. One of the first classes of cruise ships was the 19,800-ton 'Ivan Franko' class, the lead ship *Ivan Franko* entering service in 1964. With four sisterships, this Soviet vessel can accommodate 700 passengers and has a speed of 20kts.

The Soviet passenger fleet belongs to nine big shipowners in the country and the bulk of it comprises large serial ships which satisfy the growing demands of Soviet citizens for deep-sea transport and cruising, as well as catering for the foreign tourists. One of the nine shipowners is the Baltic Shipping Company and one of its passenger liners — an 'Ivan Franko' type — is the *Mikhail Lermontov*, which is popular with British holidaymakers and makes cruise voyages during the autumn and winter season between London and Las Palmas in the Canaries. Another Baltic Shipping vessel is the 1,371 dwt cargo passenger ship *Estonja*.

This trend in class or serial ships was continued by Fred Olsen in 1966, who introduced the 9,000-ton *Black Watch* and *Black Prince*. Norwegian Carribean Lines followed with the *Starward* and *Skyward* in 1968 and 1969. Royal Carribean introduced the first of the well-known Wärtsilä sisters, *Song of Norway* in 1970, followed by the *Nordic Prince* in 1977 and the *Sun Viking* in 1972. Wärtsilä also built another trio, this time for the Royal Viking Line; the *Royal Viking Star* in 1972 and the *Royal Viking Sea* and *Royal Viking Sky* in 1973.

Cunard entered the small cruise ship field after the

The American passenger liner *United States* which won the Blue Riband on her maiden voyage.   *Real Photos*

Queen Elizabeth II entered service in 1969. It took over twin vessels being built for Overseas National Airways and named them the *Cunard Adventurer* and *Ambassador*, which were eventually replaced by the *Cunard Countess* in 1976 and the *Cunard Princess* in 1977. Another pair of cruise liners were the *Sea Venture* and *Island Venture* for Friendship Cruises in 1972 and 1973. In 1974 they were sold to P&O-owned Princess Cruises and renamed as *Pacific* and *Island Princess*. Another notable series of ships are the 16,631grt 'Belorussiya' class, built by Wärtsilä during the second half of the 1970s and designated ferry/cruise liners.

A number of ships were also brought out of retirement or saved from the breakers yard in order to meet the demand for cruise liners. For instance, the former American Export Line's *Independence*, which was laid up for 10 years at Hong Kong, was purchased by American Hawaii Cruises and now sails as the *Oceanic Ind.* Another well-known liner to be given a new lease of life was the British built *Olympic*, while the major revival stories are, of course the previously mentioned transatlantic liners *France*, now in service as the *Norway*, and the *United States*, should it eventually enter cruise service.

Yet another aspect of cruise liner construction is to 'stretch' existing tonnage rather than build costly new vessels. In 1963 Finnlines extended its 5,000grt *Ilmatar* with 65ft of mid-body. The *Song of Norway* was also modified in 1978, followed by the *Nordic Prince* in 1980 and the *Royal Viking Star* in 1981. A twist on this stretching principle was the addition of a completely new upper sun terrace deck on Norwegian America's *Sagafjord*.

Some innovations have been introduced into the cruise liner market, such as the extremely well-equipped vessels *Linblad Explorer* and *World Discoverer*, which are rather small vessels and designed to cruise remote regions of the world each carrying less than 100 passengers. For these expedition-type cruises there is also the 4,000grt *Argonaut*, while Royal Viking Line's *Royal Viking Star* and *Sky* offer an all-year round series of cruises that have no regular itinerary.

Considering the design aspects of cruise ships, one important condition they have to meet is that they are able to enter small, as well as large ports, which places limitations on draught. Manoeuvrability is another factor of prime importance, as well as the requirements of large storage and storage access facilities. One natural choice of powerplant that provides flexibility of operation and economy is the medium-speed diesel. It is likely that the new generation of cruise ships, while capable of 20-22kts, will cruise for long periods at 14-18kts.

Finally, a class of passenger ship known as the Special Trade Passenger (STP) ship had its name coined at the 1971 IMCO Conference to cover the vessels hitherto known as Unberthed Passenger Ships and Pilgrim Ships. STP ships — which are designed to provide cheap travel — are engaged carrying a large number of passengers on international short-sea or even coastal voyages in dormitory-type accommodation in the upper decks and between decks, and operate predominantly in the tropical areas of the Red Sea, Arabian Sea, Indian Ocean and South China Sea. The passengers in such ships generally belong to developing countries in these regions and may be on pilgrim voyages or else are immigrants. One such vessel is the 18kts *Akbar*, built for the Mogul Line in 1971 to carry up to 1,490 unberthed pilgrims.

The *Queen Elizabeth II* was built for Cunard in 1969; now, after modifications, she is of 67,000grt. Originally intended for the Southampton-New York run, she now cruises in the winter months and served as a troopship in the task force despatched to the Falklands. *Cunard*

Canberra which also saw service as a troopship in the
Falklands.   *Real Photos*

The *Mikhail Lermontov*, one of the 'Ivan Franko' type of
Russian cruise ships.   *Baltic Shippping Co*

13

Passenger and Car Ferries

Passenger and car ferries vary a great deal in size and appearance. There are the purely passenger type craft, car ferries and train ferries. The car ferry may have cars loaded at either bow or stern ramps, or both, or by side doors, according to the convenience of the terminal ports. The train ferry is used only for a few short sea routes and has a broad beam, high superstructure and lack of sheer and derricks.

Just as air passenger transport brought about the near demise of regular passenger liner services so the increase in volume of private and commercial vehicles has similarly afflicted the passenger only ferries. Today, the car ferry is predominant on almost all major ferry routes and this chapter will be mostly concerned with such vessels.

It was the *Forde* and *Autocarrier* which pioneered the specialised carrying of vehicles in the early 1930s and the development of the car ferry then gained momentum owing to the growth of traffic with private cars and lorries. The concept reached new peaks in the postwar era as holidaymakers sought to explore new lands for their enjoyment. North-West Europe is probably the most ferry 'populated' region in the world, while the English Channel is well served with ferry services and the Mediterranean encompasses many different ferry routes. Even Japan has undergone a ferry boom, most Japanese ferries differing in design from their western counterparts.

Looking at the design aspects of car ferries, a most illustrative example of design change is seen in the profiles of typical ferries during the 1970s, where the 'wedding cake' silhouette has been replaced by types in which all the superstructure decks are utilised to the last square metre, thus presenting a very block profile.

Cars being driven on to Captain Stuart Townsend's *Forde* when the ramp at the Quai Paul Devot was used for the first time in Calais on 9 June 1936. This was during the French general strike and heralded the coming of today's modern car/passenger services.

A queue of passengers waiting to board one of the Sealink consortium's ferries. *Sealink*

The spacious foredeck of previous years is fast becoming obsolete in the search for more 'moneymaking' space, and there has been an increase in 'top weight'.

External design has also changed by introducing more through car decks; the moulded depth to the upper through deck has risen because of this, and the design ratios L/B, L/D and B/D have changed within recent years. New ferry hull forms tend — from fleet owners' requests — toward approximately rectangular car trailer decks, maximum access openings forward and aft, higher ships and increased breadth. Recently, twin hulls (split stern) have been used in ferry designs. Another owner requirement is for box-shaped car decks, which caused problems in the design of web frames.

There has been a tendency toward even larger vessels, for which the term 'super ferry' is now being used. This, combined with a desire for shorter terminal times, has put pressure on the development of ro-ro equipment for ferries in recent years. The trend is now toward stern and bow door constructions (as against the smaller side doors of the past), the ramps allowing two-way trailer traffic. Trailer and lorry traffic is a decisive part of the total earnings of most Northern European ferry services and the requirements for maximum flexibility give rise to complicated ramp systems.

Modern multi-screw ferry designs typically have diesel engine systems (main and auxiliary plants) with a tendency in the design of propulsion systems toward two or more main engines of the medium speed type. Economy of fuel consumption is another factor due to the rising costs of oil.

Patterns of travel have changed over the years and are still undergoing change; group travel, business trips, charter tours, etc, have all affected ferry accommodation arrangements. Public space areas have been

Braemar (1952). *Real Photos*

developed with a view to other possible applications such as dining room conference hall and so on. The trend is toward flexibility in accommodation designs. Modern layouts of accommodation also reveal greater symmetry than in the past.

Today, most ferry builders use prefabricated toilet/bathroom units and other factory-produced accommodation elements. Prefabricated components allow for increased profitability as a result of simplified production routines, high quality workmanship and shorter fitting-out period.

An increasing level of comfort has come about in the crews' accommodation, while environmental considerations have led to their being located on the upper decks. Office facilities tend to be centrally located. The catering side has seen efforts concentrated mainly on optimal supply systems for provisions, with extensive use being made of pre-cooked food.

Safety and fire precautions are of high priority on ferries and cover watertight subdivision, evacuation, fire protection, firefighting, navigation and a number of other factors. In general, most modern ferries are either two-compartment vessels or combined one-compartment/two-compartment vessels. New designs

Dover (1965). *Real Photos*

Doric Ferry (1962). *Real Photos*

Sealink's *St Christopher* and *St Anselm* cross in mid-Channel. *Twinflight Photographic*

The 14,400-ton *Dana Anglia* is the flagship of Denmark's DFDS line, and was delivered in 1978. *DFDS*

The *Herald of Free Enterprise*, Townsend Thoresen's 8,000-ton 'Blue Riband' ship, can carry 1,300 passengers and 350 cars. She operates on the 75-minute crossing between Dover and Calais. Her sister ship *Pride of Free Enterprise* holds the record crossing of the Channel — 52min 49sec. *Townsend Thoresen*

comply with SOLAS 74, utilising non-combustible materials in accommodation areas.

Ferries on international routes are equipped with a comprehensive arrangement of liferafts, boats, or a combination of both, as the main lifesaving equipment, the standards between different countries not differing greatly. For short international routes the standards among authorities are more varied and so this situation does not apply. A critical factor in modern ferry design being deadweight, the life-saving equipment arrangements are kept to the lowest possible weight.

Important factors in ferry design are environmental considerations, which include motions, noise and vibrations. Uncomfortable or excessive motions will cause unfavourable prejudice in passengers' minds, create problems in catering, and require more lashing down of cargo. Because of these and other aspects, roll-damping devices (tanks or fins) have become more or less standard. Noise is tackled early in the design stage

A twin-screw passenger and cargo ferry, the *Lady Chilel Jawara*, was built by Ferguson-Ailsa for the government of Gambia. *Ferguson-Ailsa*

and noisy areas are segregated from others. There is still much work to be done on the vibration of ships, including ferries, and at the moment most calculations are based on empirical results.

Some vessels of interest in the ferry field include Finnline's *Finnjet* (1977) which was the world's largest at the time of 23,000grt. It is designed to cover 600 miles every day in only 22 hours at a service speed of 30kts. It is capable of loading and unloading as many as 1,532 passengers and up to 700 cars during its short terminal time of two hours.

It is gas-turbine powered but has recently been fitted with diesels for the less onerous winter conditions which require shorter crossing times. At present the largest ferry in the world by deadweight is the 3,898 dwt (25,677 grt) *Finlandia*.

Two giant-sized ferries of the German TT Line are the *Peter Pan* and the *Nils Holgersson* which operate between Travemunde and Trelleborg. Delivered in 1974 and 1975, these 22kts ships make three sailings a day with 1,600 passengers and up to 470 cars or 45 lorries.

The jumbo ferry first came to the North Sea in 1974 with the sister ships *Norland* and *Norstar*. Operating an overnight service between Hull and Rotterdam, they each carry 1,070 cabin passengers and a large mix of cars and commercial vehicles at 18kts.

Denmark's DFDS Line took delivery of its 14,400ton flagship *Dana Anglia* in 1978, only two years after the *Dana Regina* entered service. She is capable of carrying 1,249 passengers the majority being accommodated in cabins and up to 470 cars or a mix of cars, lorries and containers.

Tor Line's *Tor Brittania* and *Tor Scandinavia* were current holders of the North Sea records in 1979, having been handed over to their owners in 1975 and 1976. These vessels maintain a service speed of 24kts and have accommodation for 756 cabin passengers with a further 512 in couchettes and a maximum capacity of 420 in the car decks.

Sealink's *St Edmund* and *Princess Beatrix* operate from Harwich to the Hook of Holland, while the *Napoleon* (1976) plies the Marseilles-Corsica route and the *Habib* (1978) operates between Tunis and Marseillies. On a more local level the *Scillonia III*, built by Appledore Shipbuilders, was designed for service between Penzance and the Scilly Isles.

14
Tugs

Tugs are the workhorses of the sea and perform a variety of towing, safety and salvage duties. Their general appearance is squat and their superstructures are comparatively high, being placed well forward to leave a clear flat deck space aft. Towing hooks or bitts are attached to the aft end of superstructure and the tow rope rides over steel hoops straddling the after deck.

The first steam tug appeared on the River Thames in 1816, while the first practical steamboat — the *Charlotte Dundas*, which was built in 1801 — operated as a tug on the Forth and Clyde Canal. As the years progressed the hull form of the tug lost the narrow-gutted look so common to many vessels in the early years of this century and took on the modern lines of the present day tug.

Tugs may be classified as either ocean-going and salvage, coastal or river and harbour, and include a wide range of vessels from the 22kts salvage tug of 11,000kW to the small towing craft that tows barges. A modern innovation in design is the anchor/handling tug which developed from the North Sea offshore industry, while yet another type of tug is the pusher tug, pioneered in the USA and now comprehensively used on US and European waterways. Stability under all conditions is a prime requirement of all tugs, along with manoeuvrability and adequate towing power. The efficiency of a tug is assessed according to the percentage power it can transmit through a tow rope to another vessel.

Ocean-going tugs spend long periods at sea and have high power, sea-going characteristics, displacement and radius of action. Modern ocean-going tugs carry sophisticated navigational equipment as well as a high standard of accommodation, extensive fuel and fuel storage capacity, salvage gear and firefighting facilities, and other hardware to enable them to operate worldwide in all conditions.

Coastal tugs are usually of medium power and short dimensions, and have a good sheer foreward to reduce the effect of heavy seas. They are also frequently fitted with a forecastle. Salvage gear and fire pumps will form a standard part of their equipment, while the accommodation is arranged to gain access to important areas of the vessel such as the bridge and engineroom without having to traverse the open deck. River and harbour tugs are restricted in length to under 30m and assist large vessels in loading and unloading, and ship-handling in rivers. A special subdivision of this class of tug is the tug-tender, which is used to disembark passengers and transport workmen.

Tugs are becoming generally more powerful and

An early postwar tug, the icebreaker *Swiatowid*. *Real Photos*

Diagram of the hydroconic tug, *Sydney Cove*, as built by P. K. Harris & Son's Appledore shipyard.

The 2,100 dwt ocean-going tug/anchor handling/supply vessel *Wimpey Seahorse* was built by Appledore Shipbuilders Ltd. *Appledore*

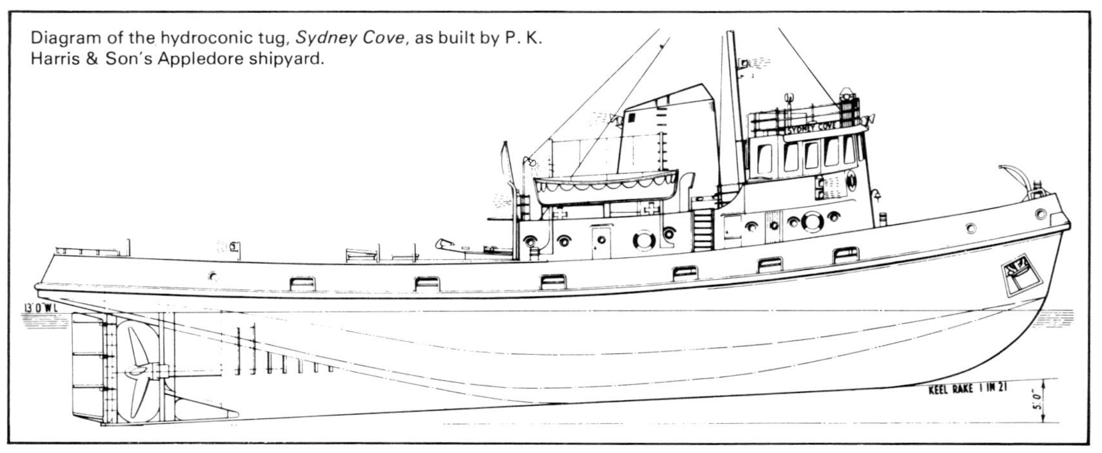

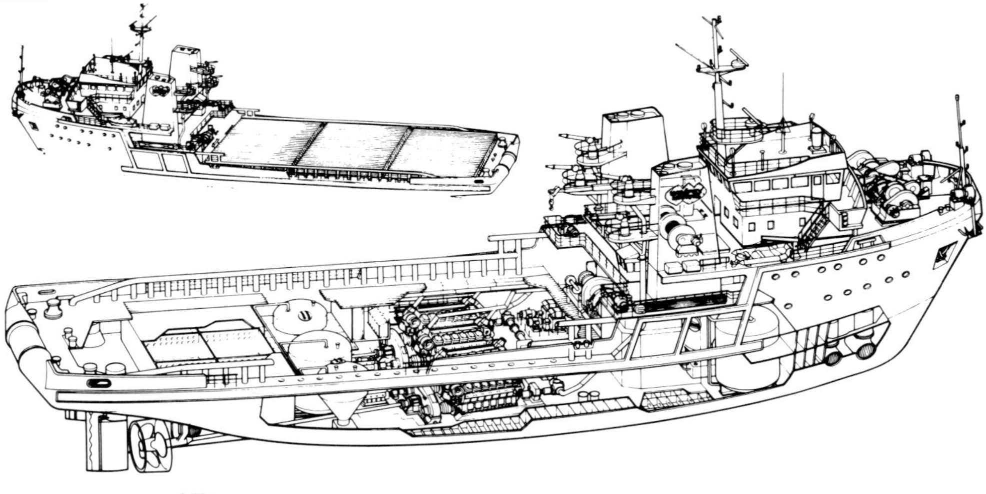

The Ferguson-Ailsa anchor handling tug/supply vessel *Seaforth Highlander*. *Ferguson-Ailsa*

versatile and a new breed of tug/supply ships has come into existence for offshore applications. Hull forms are of the hard chine or round bilge type and arguments prevail as to the merits of each form. One innovation in tug hull design and construction occurred just after World War 2 when P. K. Harris and Sons, Ltd of North Devon, constructed a new hard chine type of tug of hydroconic design, in conjunction with Seawork Ltd, who were the designers and a subsidiary of Burness, Corlett and Partners. P. K. Harris produced a number of such tugs. The company was later to become Appledore Shipbuilders Ltd. The hydroconic form was based on the expansion of a cone and a major advantage was that it provided curvature only in one direction (the longitudinal), thus allowing ease and simplicity of construction. Trawlers were also built to this form and the venture captured a large slice of the market in the 1950s.

One significant development in tug design is the Schottel Tractor Tug. Based on experience over the years of a type of tug having the propulsive units under the forebody and the towing hook abaft the midship point, Schottel developed the craft in close co-operation with experienced naval architects. This type of tug has the ability to manoeuvre equally and as fast astern as ahead, and is able to move laterally and push or pull, while turning circles and stopping distances at full power, both ahead and astern, are about one ship's length.

As in so many fields, tug design now takes into consideration the conservation of fuel. Twin engines are one answer to this, where only one engine is used when the vessel is running light. An example of this type is the *Clauseman*, built by Richards (Shipbuilders) Ltd for the Red Funnel Group. Extending this idea further, the tug *Salvageman*, built for United Towing,

has four engines driving twin screws, providing increased manoeuvrability as well as economy of operation.

Many developments have occurred in tug propulsion, machinery and fittings since 1945: for instance, Voith Schneider cycloidal propellers which provide thrust through 360°, the Schottel Rudderpropeller and other screw arrangements, Kort nozzles, which increase the thrust, and bow thrusters and featherweight controls to provide manoeuvrability and ease of handling. Modern hydraulic deck machinery and cranes are installed, as well as batteries of the most up-to-date navigational aids. Tow ropes are of either man-made materials or natural fibres such as manilla or sisal and coir. A number of patent hooks are available, all obtaining their flexibility by using a spring-loaded type hook with quick-release mechanism. Some tugs such as the *Salvageman* do not even have a hook — a far departure from the prewar concept of this type of vessel. A modern development in tug equipment is the towing winch, which controls the tension on the rope.

Looking at some tug constructions, Appledore Shipbuilders built the *Lloydsman*, which was considered the most powerful British tug at its time of delivery, having a bollard pull of 150 tons and able to tow a fully-laden 300,000 dwt tanker at 7kts. The *SA Wolraad Woltemade* was launched in 1975. Built by Robb Caledon Shipbuilders for Safmarine, this 2,020 dwt vessel was the world's most powerful tug at the time and was designed for ocean towing, rescue, firefighting, salvage and pollution control and had a bollard pull in excess of 200 tons, with a speed over 21kts. Two powerful French tugs built in 1978 were the *Abeille*

Many tugs are equipped for fire-fighting duties. In this picture
Ferguson Ailsa's *Flying Phantom* is seen using its fire pumps.
Ferguson-Ailsa

Twin engines and twin screws can provide an answer to fuel
conservation. The Ferguson-Ailsa-built tug *Holmgarth* has two
Ruston 6RK3CM engines driving twin Voith Schneider
propellers.   *Ferguson-Ailsa*

Among the developments in tug propulsion is the Schottel Rudderpropeller which can be seen under the tractor tug *Al Alliah*. *Schottel-Werft*

Schottel's tugs are in operation in the port of Hamburg and other ports worldwide: (*right*) *Janus*; (*below*) a Bugsier tug towing a drilling platform to the North Sea. *Schottel*

Ferguson-Ailsa's *Carron*, a water tractor. *Ferguson-Ailsa*

Normandy and *Abeille Provence*, having bollard pulls of 120 tons. Also in 1978 the *Wimpey Seahorse* was delivered, built by Appledore Shipbuilders, being the first of two firefighting tug/anchor-handling supply vessels built by the company. One prolific builder of tugs and other small craft is Ferguson Ailsa, and recent tug constructions by the company have been the *Carron*, *Holgarth* and *Flying Phantom*. Finally, among a number of Schottel Tractor Tug constructions is the *Al Alliah*.

15
Fishing Vessels

It is not possible to cover the numerous craft that populate the world's fishing fleet in just a chapter, but the craft that are briefly described or mentioned do broadly fall into the major categories representing the international fishing industry. A quick review is also presented of postwar developments in the UK fishing industry, along with a few other countries such as the USA. This, at least will give some idea of the changing scene of fishing.

The fishing boat — unlike other cargo-carrying vessels — has to allow for the fact that it obtains its payload from the sea, and one of the preliminary design problems is how this is to be achieved. The fishing process involves three basic methods of catching fish: towing (using trawls or dredges), surrounding nets (purse seines), or static systems (anchored nets or pots). Fishing craft will fish for pelagic (surface feeding) or demersal (bottom feeding) species, or both.

Those vessels which tow nets or dredges include side trawlers, beam trawlers and stern trawlers. In the same category can be placed 'wet' fishers or 'freshers', freezer trawlers and factory vessels. Those which use the surround method of catching can be subdivided into ones using nets with rope, such as flydraggers, Scottish seiners or anchor seiners, and ones using net only, such as purse seiners. Ringnetters also come under this general category. Vessels which use static means of fishing are potters (crabs, lobsters, etc), drifters, gillnetters and tanglenetters. In the same category can be placed liners.

The international fishing industry as a whole has grown in postwar years, very much due to an increasing world population and its food demands. In some places it has grown from being a cottage industry to a major source of food supply, while in others there have been fluctuating fortunes due to changing tastes or demands. One important event that has changed the pattern of international fishing since World War 2 is the general extension of fishing limits from the world norm of 12 miles to 200 miles. The increasing constraints placed on fishing operations, by restricting areas where vessels can work and limiting the fishing effort on any one species of fish, mean very few vessels can be so specialised as to handle only one type of gear. New designs have been produced, able to take advantage of whatever species were in season, thus sustaining their profitability throughout the year.

Considering the UK fishing industry, which fishes in areas traditionally referred to as Inshore, Near, Middle and Distant water grounds, depending on their relative position to the UK coastline. Inshore waters are normally considered to be within 12 miles of the coast, while the others extend farther, according to certain boundaries. For example, Near and Middle waters extend from 12 miles to the coast of Denmark and Holland for one boundary, while Distant waters could be as near as Iceland or as far as Labrador. The industry has suffered in some ways because of the 200-mile limit. For instance, the loss of the Icelandic fishing grounds resulted in the number of Distant water vessels declining. Other vessels had to adapt to the new conditions.

The coastal fishing vessel *Vorrbok* (1944).   *Real Photos*

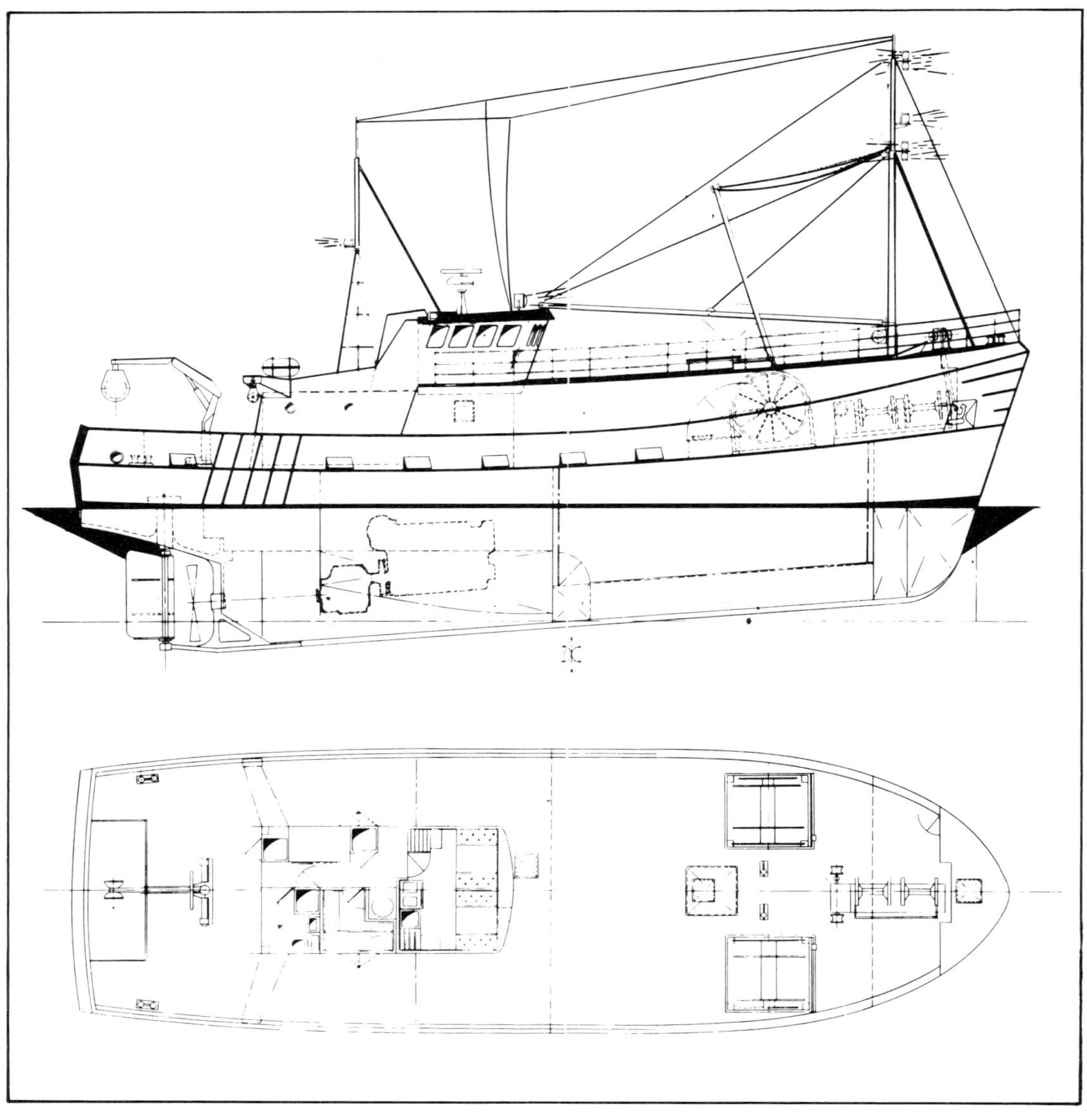

Comparison drawings of the Campbeltown 65 (*above*) and Campbeltown 85 (*right*).

Perhaps the most important fishing vessel is the trawler and UK trawlers play a significant role in the industry. They can be classified according to the areas they generally work in (as above) and range in length from an inshore water trawler — under 24.3m — to a Distant water trawler — greater than 41.23m. A further subdivision gives three basic types according to the methods of processing and preserving fish. These are freezer trawlers, 'wet' fish trawlers or 'freshers', and factory vessels. Freezer trawlers gut and freeze their catch; wet fishers store gutted fish in ice or hold fish in RSW or CSW tanks; factory vessels have the capability of also processing it to produce various products.

The trawler engages in all-the-year-round fishing and must be strong and robust in order to work in the worst of weather. The modern trawler is an efficient vessel fitted with the latest electronic equipment and gear for fishing and navigation. It has a pronounced sheer, a superstructure placed well aft and a clear forecastle deck fitted with compartments or ponds for sorting the catch. Another characteristic is the powerful winch placed just forward of the wheelhouse. A modern trawler is exemplified by the *Kestrel*, fabricated entirely under cover by the purpose-built Campbeltown shipyard and delivered to its owners in 1978. One new feature is its shelter deck, which extends well aft to allow the crew to work under cover.

A postwar development in trawlers is the stern trawler, the first versions being introduced in the early 1960s as pioneered by the 'Fairtrys' series. Instead of

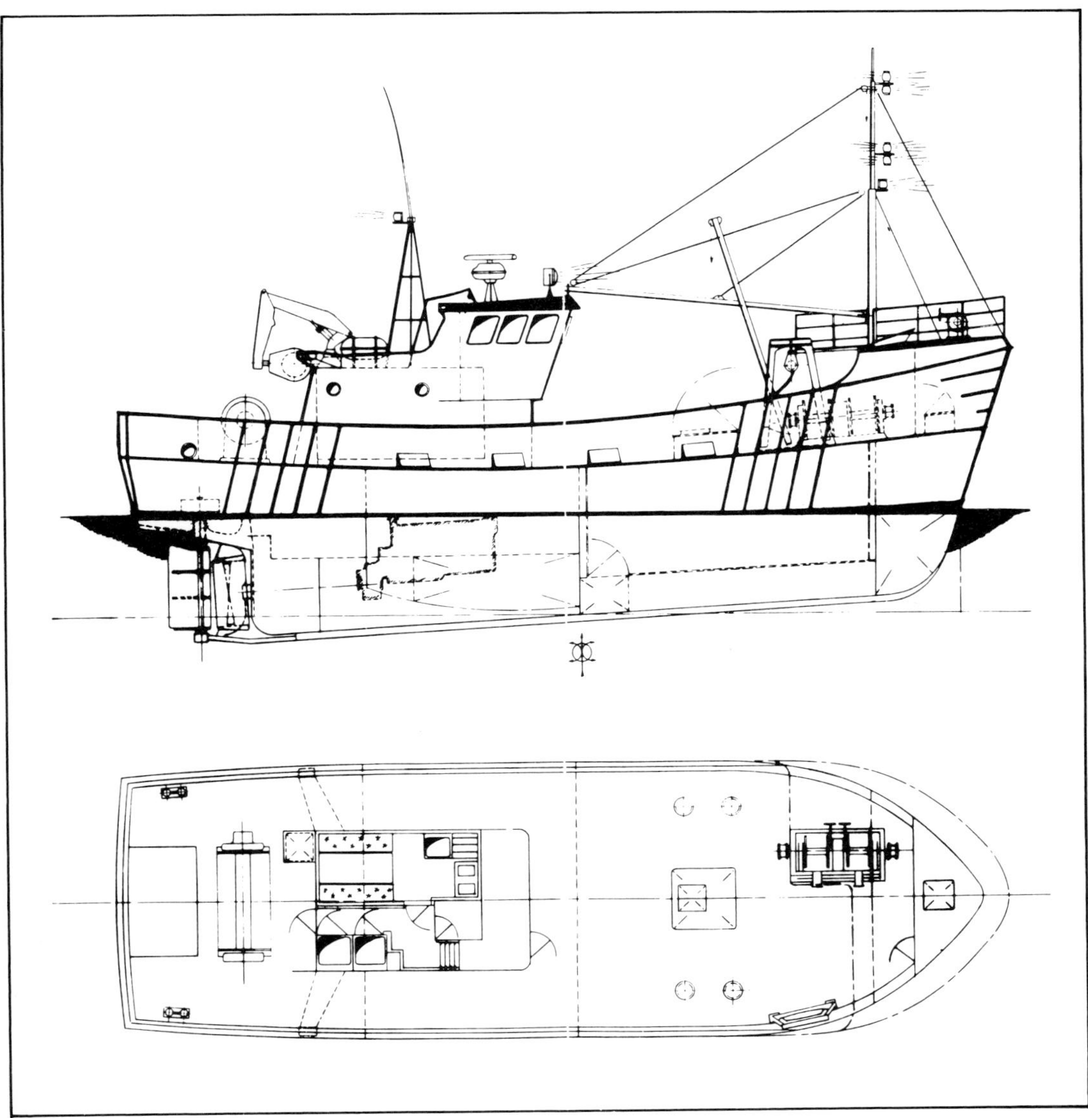

using the traditional method of hauling the net over the side at the gallows, the stern trawler hauls it over a ramp at the stern. Original designs were for demersal cod fishing off Iceland but later versions were designed to enable them to be deployed in other capacities and for longer periods. When combined with the introduction of a fish processing vessel, the stern trawler resulted in the fish factory trawler. Examples of sophisticated and versatile stern trawlers are the four vessels built by Richards (Shipbuilders) Ltd in 1978, the *Boston Sea Vixen*, *Boston Sea Cobra*, *Boston Sea Gazelle* and *Boston Sea Stallion*. The vessels were designed for demersal and pelargic fishing and the last two each have three RSW tanks and a 3-ton derrick forward of the gantry for fish handling.

The drifter is a fishing vessel that may be seen at many of Britain's smaller ports. The characteristics of the herring drifter are a powerful capstan forward, no forecastle, and hinged foremast, and a small mizzen sail to keep the vessel's head to the wind. The Scottish flydragger or seiner, which has been fishing the North Sea for approximately 45 years, had a wooden hull and a mechanical multi-geared winch in the early 1960s, but modern vessels include many developments such as a hydraulic winch and steel hull. Vessels that employ the purse seine method of fishing first entered service in the UK in the late 1960s, when existing craft were modified to suit this type of fishing, working in conjunction with a skiff. The present generation of seiners have dispensed with the function of the skiff by making use of bow thrusters among other developments, the catch transferred by means of a pump into RSW tanks.

The USA's fishing industry has gone through a period of considerable expansion, and the north-west coast of Alaska contains the majority of new fishing grounds being developed, the two main areas being king crab fishery and trawling. Much of the new design and construction is concentrated there, with purpose-built vessels being constructed combining both processing and storage facilities. The north-east US coast fisheries are most closely related to European fisheries and up to a few years ago were little more than cottage industries, supplying fish to local areas. The older trawlers are being replaced by more modern vessels, able to fish distant waters and equipped in the European fashion. The US shrimp industry is based on the Gulf coast and the craft involved are very basic. Early construction was in timber but this has largely been replaced by steel. On the California coast there is a tuna fleet, the vessels ranging up to 2,000 tons and being known as tuna clippers in recognition of the fine lines of the ships.

Russia and Japan have been involved in the whaling industry for some time and Russian and Japanese whale factory ships leave their home ports in October and spend the whole of the Antarctic summer in the whaling grounds, returning home in the early spring. The standard whale factory ship resembles a large tanker, but the bridge is usually farther forward and it has a higher freeboard, heavy derricks and kingposts. The whales are hauled up through a stern slipway on the flensing deck. World opinion now is against the whale catching industry, and bans have been imposed on whale catching by most nations.

Finnish trawlers take their biggest catches in winter by trawling through ice. There were 160 of these vessels in 1979, of which only a score or so were built of steel, a prerequisite for working in ice. This meant that a majority of the fleet were idle during the four winter months when the Baltic is iced over and the best catches can be made. When the demand for Baltic

Among new developments in fishing vessels in postwar years is the stern freezer trawler. Illustrated is the block freezer stern trawler *Roman* of 1,000 tonnes dwt. *Ferguson-Ailsa*

The whale oil factory ship *Kosmos III* (1947). *Real Photos*

The fish carrier *Refrigerator No 7* (1953). *Real Photos*

The whaler *Enern* (1952).   *Real Photos*

The fish factory ship *Davy Dov* (1963).   *Real Photos*

herring increased, one Finnish trawler owner decided to take advantage of this and had a steel trawler built with an icebreaking hull. The vessel, *Jarvsaar*, has a trawl frame of new design and a completely covered 'tweendeck'.

Fishing in Denmark has always been of an individual nature and thus, distinctive types of craft have developed. There are single-mast wooden motor cutters which fish for plaice with a seine net in the North Sea, and larger Danish fishing cutters which fish far from their home ports.

A vessel found in Spanish, French and Portugese fleets is one specially built for fishing the Newfoundland Grand Banks and is larger than the trawler. Other fishing vessels of European origin are the Pareja, Portugese sardine seiner and Portugese longliner.

16
Dredgers

Whenever it is necessary to maintain the depth of water in channels, docks and basins, dredgers perform these operations. These vessels can be divided into three traditional categories: bucket, suction and grab.

The bucket-ladder dredger has no hopper space and is not self-propelled, being moved by tugs and transferring its spoil into hopper barges. The hull has a well at centre (or sometimes at bow or stern) and a ladder fitted with an endless belt of buckets that extends to the sea bottom. As each bucket reaches the sea bottom it scoops up the spoil and carries it to the top of the ladder, where a tripping device tips the bucket up and empties the spoil down a chute into a hopper barge. One non-propelled bucket dredger is the *MSC Ince*, built for the Manchester Ship Canal Co. The suction dredger (used when the bottom is mainly sand) lowers a flexible pipe down to the sea bottom and the spoil is sucked or drawn up into the hoppers. Sometimes the nozzle at the end of the suction pipe is fitted with a revolving cutter to break up certain grounds. A typical suction hopper dredger is the *Sand Weaver* while another is the *Baglan*, both built by Ferguson Ailsa.

The grab dredger in its simplest form is a pontoon with a slewing and hoisting crane capable of operating a double-chain grab. Similar to other dredgers, it may transfer its spoil to hoppers. The dipper dredger is a large pontoon with a heavy crane and dipper gear at one end. The dipper gear consists of a shovel which is lowered into the water to excavate the bottom. The spoil is then transferred to a hopper. This dredger — which has no hopper or propelling machinery — lowers legs or spuds on to the seabed to prevent movement while dredging is in progress.

Converted coasters or barges, equipped with dredging grab cranes, were the first to recover aggregate from the sea. The *Arco Thames* is typical of a self-unloading aggregate dredger, one of the modern innovations in sand dredgers.

The very first steam-powered dredger was a bag and spoon type, constructed in Sunderland in 1797. It was the diesel engine which stimulated a major advance in dredger development, and the majority of new dredger structures in the past 40 years have been diesel-powered.

The 19th century brought about a major division of dredger types into mechanical and hydraulic. Bucket-ladder dredgers were the first to be mechanically driven, while the development of the centrifugal pump and its adaption to sand dredging led to the introduction of the trailer and cutter-suction units. Suction dredgers now cover the widest variety of type and size, including the new generation of walking and semi-submersibles. In fact, the world's first walking cutter-suction dredger was the *Al Wassl Bay*.

Cutter-suction dredgers are best known in the construction industry because they are the most versatile. More research and development has gone into these types than into any other. Cutter-suction dredgers can now economically pump a variety of materials ranging from soft silt to medium rock.

To obtain an idea of the considerable technical advances made, the design and construction of trailing hopper suction dredgers 20 or so years ago had a capacity of 2,000cu m, which was considered substantial. Nowadays, twin chopper dredgers are around 10,000cu m capacity. Modern cutter-suction dredgers such as the semi-submersible, *Simon Stevin*, launched in December 1979, can be very sophisticated. This vessel has a permanent crew of 50 and 35,000 installed horsepower. Monitoring systems maintain the vessel exactly on course and speed, analyse the solid/water content and hold the drag heads at exactly the right depth.

Two of the largest diesel-electric cutter suction dredgers are the *Suez* and *Suraga*, which were built in Japan, and have a pump capacity of 10,000cu m per

Geopotes VII (1963). *Real Photos*

A non-propelled bucket dredger, the *MSC Ince*, built for the Manchester Ship Canal Co.

Hoveringham VI (1971).   *Real Photos*

Two Ferguson-Ailsa suction hopper dredgers: (*top*) the *Sand Weaver* and (*above*) the *Baglan*.   Ferguson-Ailsa

hour. They were employed in 1977 on the vast Suez Canal expansion programme.

The recovery of offshore minerals from deeper depths has produced dredgers capable of working at these depths. One such vessel is the *Jim Beam* which can dredge to 38m with the addition of a second pump to the ladder. The Japanese-built *Ajiago* jet ejector is designed to work at 100m, while the Dejima suction dredger — the world's largest dumb dredger — has a dredging depth of 85m, which is obtained by mounting the pump on the articulated ladder and backing it up with jet and dilution pumps.

Grab dredgers are rugged and long-lasting, but to some extent have been replaced by suction dredgers for maintenance work on sand bars and channels, although the grabs are still supreme inside harbours and docks. In recent years units with 50m booms and 40-tonne grab capacities have been built; these can also be quickly rigged as floating cranes and pile drivers. Dipper dredgers have in the past two decades or so been replaced by 360° hydraulic backhoes, which have proved superior to the former. The largest land and water-based 360° excavator in the world — the O&K RH300 — can reach down 27m and still carry a 15cu m bucket.

Three new hopper dredgers of different sizes and mission performances were under construction for the US Army Corps of Engineers and were designed to be capable of operating on all coasts and available on short notice for national defence needs or military or civilian emergencies. The dredgers incorporated a number of innovations that departed from previous practices, including the location of the entire super-structure aft and extensive automation of dredging machinery and equipment.

Within the hopper dredger category is the split hopper barge, a unique vessel type that is hinged at deck and opens up to discharge its spoil.

17
Offshore Vessels

The Gulf of Mexico was one of the first areas in the world to be explored for offshore oil. In 1947 the oil really began to flow from that part of the globe and since then offshore exploration and exploitation all over the world has burgeoned, with one of the greatest pioneering areas being in the North Sea. This relatively shallow arm of water that projects from its parent ocean, the Atlantic, has a ferocious surface and an equally horrendous underbelly. It has an average depth of only 180ft but its deepest part is 2,165ft, and its bleak face presents one of the world's coldest and most open areas of water, where 125mph easterly winds furrow its surface into 100ft high waves. It is here and in other parts of the globe that since World War 2 a gigantic offshore venture to tap the oil under the waters has been initiated. In the wake of this massive operation there has sprung up an important and new branch of the marine industry — offshore vessels. A variety of offshore craft have been designed to meet the multifarious tasks involved in offshore exploration and production — including drilling units, offshore support vessels, pipe-laying barges, etc. Each of these vessels has a history of development not possible to describe within the confines of this chapter, consequently only major offshore types will be highlighted while others will be given passing mention.

Starting with drilling units, there are generally three types: the jack-up barge, the drillship and the semi-submersible drilling rig. Each is designed to operate within certain depths and marine conditions. The first type of drilling vessel was an unpowered flat-bottomed barge with a ship-shaped hull. These were used for drilling in shallow waters and had a displacement of some 3,500 tons, although a few over 10,000 tons have been constructed. Following on these came the jack-up barge or drilling unit.

The jack-up barge is a type of drilling rig designed to operate in shallow water, generally less than 110m deep. It has a barge-like hull which may be ship-shaped, triangular, rectangular or irregularly shaped and is supported on a number of lattice or tubular legs which rest on the sea bed and provide a stable platform. Most jack-ups have three, four or five legs but a few of the earlier models had eight or 10 legs and one had 14. When the rig is being towed to a drilling location the legs are raised, projecting only a few metres below the deck. On arrival, the legs are lowered to the sea bed by electric or hydraulic jacks. The jack-up rig still forms a large part of the world's drilling fleet.

For drilling in deeper and more open water there is the semi-submersible drilling unit, which is a floating drilling rig consisting of hulls or caissons carrying a number of vertical stabilising columns, supporting a deck fitted with a derrick and associated drilling equipment. These drilling rigs differ principally in their displacement, hull configuration, and the number of stabilising columns. Most modern types have a rectangular deck; a few are cruciform-shaped, others are pentagon-shaped. The most usual hull arrangement is a pair of parallel rectangular pontoons, which may be blunt or rounded and house thrusters for position-keeping or self-propulsion. Semi-submersibles have a capability of drilling in waters up to 200m deep but some can work in 500m with the aid of dynamic positioning equipment. When under tow the semi-submersible is ballasted slightly to a depth of about 6-8m; when drilling, this is increased to 20-25m.

Looking at some recent semi-submersible rigs, the heaviest to be built anywhere in the world when it was delivered in 1981 was the *Dyvi Delta*. Suitable for drilling in waves up to 20m high, it had a steel weight of about 16,000 tonnes. The world's largest rig will be a vessel for Zapata Offshore, to be built by Kawasaka

The drilling rig *Bendora*.

The launch of semi-submersible drilling rig *Iolair* built by Scott Lithgow. It is considered to be one of the most complex merchant ships ever built.   *Scott Lithgow*

Heavy Industries and due for delivery in late 1983. A conical drilling rig has been ordered by Gulf Canada Resources, due for delivery in early 1983. It has a diameter of 81m and will operate in the Beaufort Sea. Finally, a recent UK-built semi-submersible drilling rig is the *Iolair*, built by Scott-Lithgow and considered the most complex merchant vessel ever built. It was undergoing trials in 1982, before being employed on the BP Forties Field and BNOC Thistle Field. This vessel is only the second of its breed ever to be built on the British mainland. It has a deep deck structure plus double bottom box girder construction.

Drillships — which are true ships — are specially constructed or converted for drilling for oil or gas in deep waters. Modern multi-purpose ships are fitted with dynamic positioning equipment and are able to manoeuvre accurately with the aid of thrusters fitted with controllable-pitch propellers. The drilling slot on a drillship is through the centre of gravity, while the derrick mounted above it gives the ship its distinctive appearance. Drillships range from a modest 500 dwt to over 36,000 dwt and their storage capacity enables them to dispense with service or supply ships. The drillship has a number of advantages over other drilling units when the requirement is for exploration drilling. It has independence from anchoring systems, a high transit speed and a large stores capacity.

One special type of drillship was the *Glomar*

Challenger, owned by Global Marine and able to drill in any depth of water anywhere in the world. The first UK-built drillship was the *Ben Ocean Lancer*. This 16,674-ton vessel was built by Scott-Lithgow and had a drilling capability of 10,000m. IHI Gusto BV was one of the more prolific designers and builders of such vessels in the 1970s and its first example was the *Pelican*, delivered in 1972. One of the latest is the *Polly Bristol*, delivered in 1978 after being laid up since its launch in 1976 due to a cancelled contract. The vessel has full DP capability and an eight-point mooring system.

Along with the crop of production platforms that has sprung up in offshore areas around the world has also emerged a variety of offshore support craft such as service boats, supply boats and diving support vessels. Early vessels were mostly conversions but the specialist services required for offshore platforms and construction projects soon brought about tailormade designs. Such vessels are called upon for towing, anchor-handling, transportation of supplies, hauling heavy equipment, supporting offshore operations such as pipelaying and diving, and standby duties attending offshore rigs and platforms.

Structurally, the vessels are long, wide-beamed ships of shallow draught, with the bridge well forward and a deep well extending to the stern for the carriage of pipes and other bulky equipment. Some of them are able to keep station in support of pipelaying operations; others have diving systems built into them. One such vessel is the diving barge.

The diving barge is a ship specially outfitted to support diving operations, particularly saturation diving, and may be assisted by a supply ship in the process. The diving barge provides accommodation, mooring facilities, a compressed air supply, maintenance workshops and a helipad, in addition to such special diving requirements as a saturation diving system, complete with compression/decompression chamber.

The trend now is for multi-purpose diving support ships, which have evolved from first, second and even third generation ships.

Some examples of multi-purpose diving support vessels in recent years are the *Ocean Endeavour*, a 914 dwt craft with worldwide operational capability, and carrying hyperbaric welding equipment, TV monitoring equipment and non-destructive testing (NDT) facilities as part of its hardware; the *Seaforth Clansman*, an undersea support vessel, was launched in 1977, having a saturation diving system and moon pool; and the *Seabex*, a diving support vessel with advanced station keeping capability which was delivered to its owners in 1978. A very recent version of such vessels is the *Star Hercules*, completed in 1980 by Appledore Shipbuilders for its owners, Star Offshore Services. This particularly sophisticated and versatile offshore ship is equipped for pipe-carrying and general supply duties, with provision being made for diving support. She is also equipped with a moonpool, dynamic positioning and a four-point mooring system, helium gas cylinders and other facilities for future sub-sea and saturated diving operations.

In connection with undersea activities, a breed of submersibles has been developed to perform work ranging from oceanographic survey to installation,

The Scott Lithgow-built *Ben Ocean Lancer* (*above*) and (*right*) a view showing its helicopter deck. Helicopters play a major role in the oil production business for offshore vessels.
Scott Lithgow

inspection and recovery of sub-sea equipment such as wellheads and submarine pipelines. There are two basic types of submersible; one which conforms to the conventional submarine form in which work is done from within the hull by means of a series of hydraulic manipulators, and the diver lock-out submersible, which is a sub-sea habitat for divers working on the sea bed. Such underwater vehicles usually have a crew of two or three, and a variation of the former is telechiric, which is the operation of an unmanned tethered vehicle by cable control from the surface. This type of vehicle is equipped with a 'human hand' mechanism. An example of a lock-out submersible is Vickers Oceanics 'L' class diver lockout vessel. Submersibles can operate at great depths and may be self-propelled by electric motors. They are usually assisted by a mother ship which provides workshop facilities and search and navigation services.

The laying of submarine pipelines is an important part of offshore operations and there are specially designed vessels for this purpose. First there is the pipe barge, which has a long wide well at stern and is used to carry large diameter pipes in support of submarine pipelaying operations, transporting the pipes from the supply base to the pipelaying barge. The pipelaying barge — or more commonly, the lay barge — is developed specifically for offshore pipelaying opera-

Offshore support craft: *Oil Prospector*

Offshore support craft: *Oil Endeavour*

tions. Early types were modified flat-bottomed barges only capable of laying one or two kilometres of pipe a day. They had to suspend operations even in moderate seas. Modern barges are designed on the ship or semi-submersible style and are more stable in rough seas than conventional barges. Such vessels are floating workshops having as many as six welding stations on deck, making it possible to line-up, weld, X-ray and lay continuously at a fast rate. They have a stinger (a long cambered arm) hinged at stern to act as a catenary supporting the welded run of pipe before it is laid on the sea bed.

An ancillary vessel to pipelaying operations is the bury barge, which is specially equipped to perform the last operation in the laying of a submarine pipeline. After the pipe is laid on the sea bed and positioned, a sled is towed alongside it by the bury barge. As it proceeds along the line so jets of water are directed at high pressure into the sand, scouring away the sea bed and thus permitting the pipe to settle into the trench so formed. The sand is collected by suction hoses and discharged into the sea. Depending on the composition of the sea bed, a pipe can be sunk into a trench one metre deep by this method.

Of course, many developments have occurred for specialist offshore services and operations, and the above gives only a picture of the offshore scene and its marine back-up, possibly leaving out a number of up-to-date designs.

Supply vessels at BP's Marine Base, Dundee. *BP*

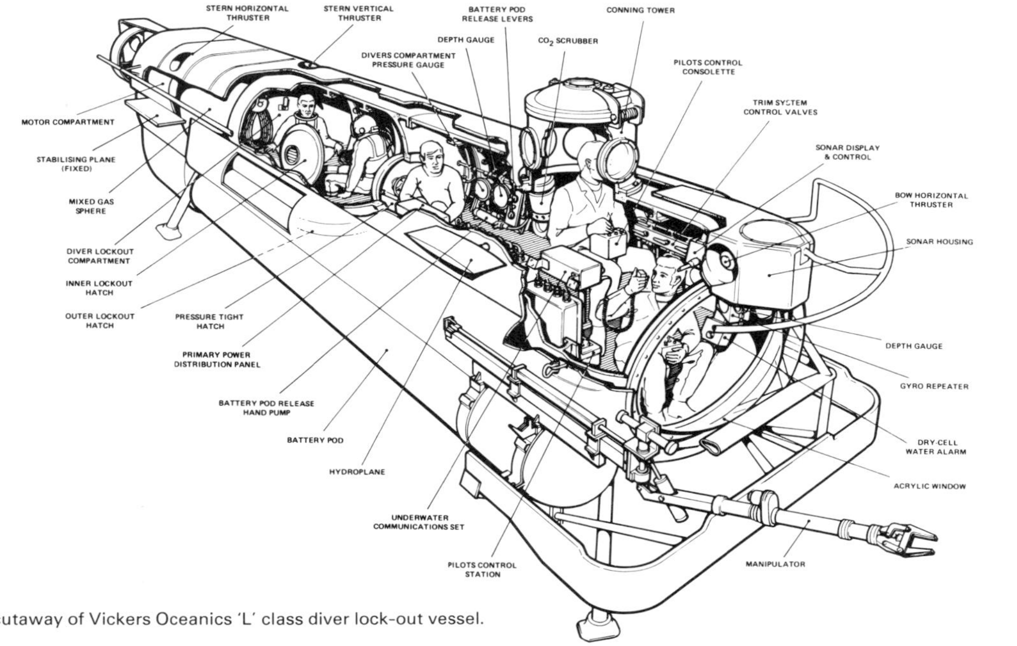

A cutaway of Vickers Oceanics 'L' class diver lock-out vessel.

18

Hydrofoils and Hovering Craft

The hydrofoil concept has, in principle, been known a long time. The first known hydrofoil — by Thomas Moy — ran down the Surrey Canal, London, in 1861, yet it is only in recent years that the idea has been developed and applied commercially. The world's first passenger hydrofoil service started only 24 years ago with the *Supramar* PT10 operating on Lake Maggiore. Since then, this mode of travel has spread to well over 40 countries and carries millions of passengers annually.

The hull geometry of a hydrofoil is almost inevitably of a slender enough form to minimise wavemaking resistance, with a V-shaped hard-chine underwater section. Many hulls are stepped on the underside to assist 'take-off'. At full speed the best hull shape would probably be similar to an aircraft fuselage, but the underside of hull obviously needs to be profiled for good hydrodynamic performance.

The *raison d'etre* for the hydrofoil is primarily the much greater lift force obtained compared to that for a flat or nearly flat planing surface; at 3° trim and 40kts the fully submerged hydrofoil ideally produces about $6\frac{1}{2}$ times the lift of the same planing surface, and has a 20% superiority in lift/drag ratio.

Looking at the basic theory, the hydrofoils operate like the wing of an aircraft. There is a reduction in pressure on the upper surface of the foil which produces the lift force. Comparison of a hydrofoil's foils with an aircraft wing shows that it is very much smaller; this is because the given area of foil in seawater can support about 800 times that of an efficient wing of similar area, moving in air at similar speeds at sea-level.

The shape of the foil in plan is seldom critical, but compared with aircraft wings they tend to be shorter and stubbier as a result of their high loading. The foil structure has to be extremely strong to absorb this high loading. When the hull is clear of the water the lift is constant, which means that with increased speed the angle of incidence must be reduced or the immersed area of foil reduced. This leads to two basic types of foil systems: (a) surface-piercing foils and (b) completely submerged, incidence-controlled foils (see Fig 1).

Surface-piercing foils can be either vee-foils or hoops, or surface-piercing ladder foils where equilibrium is maintained by a bodily rise or sinkage of the craft as it alters speed. Alexander Bell's *Hydrodome* (1918), which reached a record-breaking speed of 70.86mph on its ladder foils, and von Schertel's 1936 design with hoop foils in tandem, are early examples of this type. For practical application the scheme patented by Schertel and Sachsenberg has been installed in over 120 craft, whereas ladder foils are seldom used today.

For fully-submerged incidence-controlled foils, the foils always remain submerged and the lift generated is varied by controlling the angle of incidence of the foils. This type of foil is unaware of the presence of the wave surface, except through the action of the orbital motions of the wave particles. It was an Englishman, Christopher Hook, who first became aware that a hydrofoil was wanted that could 'feel' the pressure of oncoming waves and use this information to feed into a control system that would adjust the foils appropriately. A modern example of this type is the *Boeing Jetfoil*.

There are two options available in powerplants for hydrofoils: diesel engines and gas turbines. There are two modes of propulsion which can provide the necessary thrust: the screw propeller and the waterjet. The decisions influencing choice are not simple — any more than with a conventional ship. While air pro-

Fig 1 Basic foil geometrics. **Fig 2** ACV arrangements: (A) plenum chamber; (B) peripheral jet principle; (C) flexible skirt; (D) rigid sidewalls.

pellers, marine screws or waterjets can be used as the propulsive mechanism for a hydrofoil, conventional marine screw propellers have been used for the vast majority of hydrofoils, being efficient over the important speeds of from 12 to 70mph range. For higher speeds the supercavitating propeller is one answer, accepting the fact it will have lower efficiency, especially at lower speeds.

When it comes to materials, aluminium alloy has been used extensively, while a few craft have even had steel hulls. The weight of craft is integrally related to the power requirements and there is always unremitting pressure to reduce structural weight. Like alloy, GRP has a good weight/strength ratio and hydrofoil builders are seriously looking at this material.

Russia has led the field in hydrofoil construction, where the sheltered rivers and lakes of the country make such vessels ideal to use. In November 1961 the Gorki yard launched the *Sputnik*; this 121-ton vessel was a landmark in hydrofoil construction at the time, carrying 300 passengers on her maiden voyage.

Many hydrofoils have been constructed for military reasons, such as the PHM-1 *USS Pegasus*, including such tasks as beach assault roles, landing craft and patrol vessels. They have also entered the pleasure boat arena. Looking at some modern commericial hydrofoils, one well-known design is the PT.50, which operates in Norway and Australia among other places worldwide, including the River Plate. The Italian shipyard Navaltechnica in Messina is very much involved in the design and construction of hydrofoils, having a range of high speed surface-piercing craft from the RHS70, passenger capacity 70, up to RHS160, with passenger capacity up to 180 and the RHS200, passenger capacity 220 and up to 262 on commuter routes.

There are two types of powerplant available for hydrofoils: diesel engine or gas turbine. For example (*above*), this MTU 16V538 diesel engine is one of a range of '538' series engines used on high speed craft for high performance operations and (*below*) the Detroit Diesel Allison free turbine model 570-K. *MTU; Detroit Diesel*

Hydrofoils are powered by either screws or waterjets. Illustrated is the Rockwell International Powerjet 20, a lightweight single-stage axial flow pump and one of a series of waterjet propulsion systems built by Rocketdyre and used on board the Boeing Jetfoil. *Rockwell International*

Finally, there is the well-known *Boeing Jetfoil*, an advanced design high-speed hydrofoil developed to provide commercial competitive transport on either protected or open ocean water routes. Since they began operation in April 1975 Jetfoils have carried millions of passengers in service on the waterways of four continents. One such service is the inter-island run in the Hawaiian Islands, where the *Kamehameha* is in operation. The Jetfoil has also been on a cross-Channel service from Brighton and London. The boat can accommodate anything from 263 to 420 seats, depending on the configuration, while normal cruising speed is 41-43kts.

The attention is now turned to those visually flight-defying craft, ground effect machines or hovercraft. The debate still rages whether they are true aircraft or some hybrid of land, sea and air. There are a number of names and initials (besides the two mentioned) to describe the variety of vehicles designed on the hover-

craft principle and common ones in use are air cushion vehicle (ACV), captured air bubble (CAB), and air slider.

There are two main categories of ground effect machines: those that are truly amphibious (moving over any surface), and those that are for marine use only. It is also possible to categorise most GEMs as either depending on viscous flow, or not (see Fig 2). The former category (predominantly viscous flow) has very small ground clearance and requires a smooth surface over which to operate; the latter (non-viscous flow) is of interest to the naval architect, and the hovercraft is one example of this.

The basic principle underlying any GEM is the generation of a cushion of air between its undersurface and the surface over which it operates, so that relatively low power is required to propel the vehicle forward at high speed. The air pressure in the cushion is higher than ambient pressure, so an upward lift is generated that counterbalances the vehicle weight, except that part balanced by aerodynamic lift generated by the forward movement of the vehicle.

It was in May 1959 that the SRN1 first slid over English soil supported by a cushion of air, and was technically described as a peripheral-jet air-cushion vehicle. Many inventors had proposed ACVs before, but it was an Englishman, Christopher Cockerell, who first made them a reality, originally demonstrating the idea with a coffee tin experiment.

Early air-cushion developers had considered vehicles with a plenum chamber (see Fig 2), which could raise themselves off flat ground but could not clear obstacles or hover with stability. Cockerell's suggestion was for air to be pumped in all around the periphery of the underside, through a narrow slit, with the 'curtain' of air sloping sharply inwards (see Fig 2) to provide the peripheral-jet principle. By this method the air cushion is reinforced, but at the same time the acute angle of escape for such air as does escape means the escaping air presses against the cushion, keeping it well above atmospheric pressure.

The air gap was very small (only a few inches above the ground), and although there was now capability for horizontal movement, this was severely limited to surfaces that were comparatively smooth and flat. An ingenious idea overcame this problem; it was the flexible skirt. Although derided at first, it was tested on the SRN1 with great success, riding over obstacles

Hydrofoils have some military significance and the USA Navy has been in the forefront of research with its PHM-1 USS *Pegasus*.

higher than a metre and thus opening up new possibilities. It also brought the plenum chamber ACV back in the running, where the introduction of a long, outer flexible wall solved a number of the original problems. Fig 2 shows an example of this type.

The Denny D-1 testcraft built to evaluate the Wheatland recirculating seal concept can be said to be the first of what are known as surface effect ships (SES), incorporating many of the present features. It was designed only for operation in a seaway and had rigid sidewalls. From this juncture ACV development proceeded along two paths: amphibious craft and surface effect ships. The US Navy has put forward the 3000-LT Surface Effect Ship (3KSES) Programme to test the feasibility of SES technology for large ocean-going vessels.

Of the many methods of sealing the periphery of an air cushion, two principal forms have emerged: the peripheral flexible skirt, with or without internal subdivisions, and the combination of sidewall and flexible skirt. A skirt is applied to a craft for the fundamental object of increasing the clearance between the rigid parts of structure and the operating surface, and should seal the cushion with minimum loss of air. Sidewalls seal the air cushion along the sides, also with minimum loss of air but at the expense of increased drag.

A skirt will be in segments so that the only segments in the way of any protrusions will deflect, and the skirt has the form of a bag running right around the ACV's lower periphery, being of concave shape on the cushion side. Many forms of skirt have evolved, mainly based on the bag and segment concept. Skirt development has extended to the multi-skirt concept and also the multi-cushion.

Sidewalls principally function to seal the air cushion, but may also provide up to 10% of the vehicle weight when it is supported by the cushion. In the off-cushion mode they are normally capable of taking the full weight by buoyancy support. Unfortunately, they also carry the penalty of hydrodynamic drag.

The basic requirement of lift is that a cushion of air be created to support the vehicle at a certain height. This requires a large intake — often influencing the overall design — and these intakes may be forward facing or rearward facing. They may be modified by various arrangements such as rectangular slit intakes, and the most common practice for positioning air

An advanced design of hydrofoil, the Boeing Jetfoil started operations in 1975. Illustrated is the *Kamehameha* in service on inter-island runs in the Hawaiian Islands.

cushion intakes is on the upper surface. Ducting is an important element of the intake system and needs to be designed to ensure smooth air flow, as well as bringing flow to the required cross-section.

Air-propelled hovercraft often employ airscrews for lift while amphibious craft — having large air requirements — employ large fans mounted on vertical axes. Centrifugal or axial-flow fans are presently used in most hovercraft and typical cushion pressures range from 15-80lb ft/sq ft.

The propulsive device for an amphibious craft seems obviously to be an aircraft propeller; early craft used existing propellers that tended to be noisy and expensive, with poor reverse thrust among other disadvantages. High rotational tip speeds create objectionable noise problems, yet to maintain thrust while running at low speed requires a radical change of blade design. Certain studies made on 'very quiet' air propellers have produced encouraging results.

The Super-4 car ferry *Princess Anne*, the world's largest hovercraft and a direct development of BHC's SRN4. This type of vessel has carried nearly 12 million passengers and two million vehicles on over 80,000 Channel crossings since entering service. *BHC*

The marine screw propeller seems the natural selection for non-amphibious or marine craft. Its efficiency is excellent but this propulsive device does suffer from cavitation problems above approximately 30kts, and loss of efficiency above 70kts. Ducted propellers can provide maximum thrust benefits for a fixed propeller diameter, and also noise abatement, but there is significant duct drag at high speeds that can offset any gains. There is also the waterjet for marine and sidewall craft, while the centrifugal fan low-speed air-jet propulsion system offers possibilities for small craft. High-exit velocity turbojets appear to be quite impractical for air cushion vehicles due to their low propulsive efficiency at the speeds considered.

A hovercraft or GEM needs to generate power for cushion lift, propulsion and control. It may also have to power ancillary systems. The lift power for peripheral-skirted craft ranges from 35-45shp/ton (gross weight), and for sidewall craft, 10-20shp/ton. Propulsive power for the former uses about 40-50shp/ton (gross weight), while for the latter it is about 30-40shp/ton. Power requirements for direction and control may equal or even exceed that for propulsion in a number of cases.

The two main contenders to supply the foregoing power are the gas turbine — which is almost certain to be a marinised version of an aircraft engine — and the diesel engine. The gas turbine seems more suitable for commercial applications; the diesel engine — and also the petrol engine — seem the more likely choice for smaller craft.

The design of hovercraft is intrinsically bound up with a number of factors, including planform geometry, surface of operation, resistances acting, etc. The length/beam ratio is important in connection with induced drag, roll stability and, for sidewall craft, the sidewall drag at cruising speed. For passenger craft the seating width and pitch enter the geometric problem. For powering requirements and strength, the amount and distribution of payload is another factor. Efficient loading and unloading arrangements to attain

rapid turnaround time is a significant economic consideration for passenger craft.

The basic form of the hovercraft — which is platform-shaped — lends itself well to the provision of adequate buoyancy. In the majority of craft the structural platform is a multi-cell buoyancy chamber, well able to sustain damage without sinking or overturning. Weight is at a premium in the designs of ACVs and a hybrid of materials may be used to achieve light weight, among these being aluminium alloy and GRP.

Turning to present day commercial hovercraft, a world leader in the design and construction of ACVs is the British Hovercraft Corporation (BHC), which is situated on 60 acres of prime waterfront at East Cowes, Isle of Wight. BHC — which is a wholly owned subsidiary of Westland Aircraft Ltd — had its beginnings in 1830 when Moses Saunders opened a boatyard on the Thames. Through the years the company's name has changed and at one time it was involved in the design and development of large flying boats before entering into helicopters, fixed wing and missile production, which is now a large part of its business.

BHC started hovercraft work in 1958 in conjunction with the National Research and Development Council (NRDC) and built the world's first successful man-carrying hovercraft, SRN1, in 1959. Since then it has progressively designed seven types, the largest being the 300-ton Super-4 car ferry — the world's largest hovercraft — carrying up to 60 cars and 418 passengers. Two such craft — the *Princess Anne* and *Princess Margaret* are operating on the short English Channel routes, together with four 200 ton versions. The Super-4 is a direct development of BHC's SRN4 and travels over waves on a 3m deep cushion of air at speeds of up to 65kts. SRN4s have carried nearly 12 million passengers and two million vehicles on over 80,000 Channel crossings.

Other BHC hovercraft designs include the the SRN2, SRN3 and the latest development of the SRN6 'Winchester' class amphibious hovercraft, the Mk 6. Finally there is BHC's latest design, the AP1-88, a general purpose vessel able to carry 60-88 passengers at 55kts. It is a new concept in hovercraft, with a welded aluminium structure and diesel engines.

BHC's Mk 6 'Winchester' class amphibious hovercraft is the latest development of the SRN6 and here shows its climbing abilities. *BHC*

An aerial view of a BHC hovercraft at its terminal showing the
slipway. *BHC*

BHC's latest hovercraft, the AP 188, a general purpose craft
with a passenger capacity of 60-88 at 55kts. It is a new
concept in hovercraft design, with welded aluminium structure
and diesel engines. *BHC*

19
Miscellaneous

Ships covered under this chapter are those that are unique or unusual either because they perform very specialist functions, have unconventional powering systems or hull designs, or use materials of construction not normally related to marine purposes. Obviously, it will be impossible to cover the whole range of marine 'oddities', so a selected range of ships are given.

Unusual Power Sources

The first consideration is in new ways of powering that have emerged in postwar years. A number of these have been brought about because of the greater awareness of the limitedness of the world's fossil fuels, particularly oil. This has been emphasised by the regular and significant price rises in petroleum and its by-products over the past decade or so, in many cases doubling or trebling fuel costs within a short span of time. But the first — and futuristic — innovative form of marine powering for merchant vessels to consider is the result of wartime research — atomic power.

Nuclear power seems to offer almost limitless energy for ships to traverse the globe without the need to refuel. But there are still problems associated with handling and adapting this power for marine use, not disregarding the danger elements, and so far only a small minority of merchant ships are nuclear-powered. A report on the nuclear merchant ship published in 1976 dealt with basic design concepts of the marine reactor and put forward the most likely reactors developed for civil power that had been considered over the years for application to marine propulsion. These were: the pressurised water reactor, the organic liquids moderated reactor, the steam-generating heavy water reactor and the boiling water reactor. The Watt Committee on marine transport, assembled in 1976, concluded that large numbers of nuclear-powered ships were unlikely unless research and development could lead to smaller systems than at present envisaged, but earlier that year a considerable stir was caused in marine and shipping circles when the Chairman of Globtik Tankers signed a letter of intent to build three 587,653 dwt nuclear-powered tankers, being convinced that such tankers of that size and upwards were an economic proposition.

The Japanese nuclear-powered IHI-built *Mutsu*, of 8,200 dwt. *IHI*

An early postwar cable ship, the *Recorder* (1954).
Real Photos

Of the nuclear-powered merchant ships already built, the world's first was the American *Savannah*. Germany has built the *Otto Hanh* while Japan's first and only nuclear ship, the 8,200 dwt *Mutsu*, unfortunately had leakage problems at one time. The Russians have three nuclear-powered icebreakers, the *Lenin*, *Arktika* and *Sibir*, and hope to build larger vessels in future, including a gaslighter.

Coal is another source of power that has recently been revived. An updated study by Y-ARD Ltd in 1980 was concerned with the viability of coal-fired Panamax bulk carriers, concluding that a 60,000 dwt ship of 16,650bhp and an operating range of 10,000nm would best illustrate coal's attractiveness as a fuel. Marine steam turbine technology is certainly adequate for working in conjunction with the coal burning fluidised bed boiler and the evidence suggests that the economics favour such a means of powering.

Other alternative fuels have been, and still are being considered, such as synthetic oil, which can be produced from coal and natural gas; hydrogen, which to produce from non-fossil sources requires heat or electricity from nuclear sources; methane, which is potentially attractive because it is a liquid at ambient temperature and pressure, and is produced from coal or natural gas or may be synthesised from limestone or air using nuclear-generated electricity; ammonia, considered a synthetic fuel on the basis that it could be manufactured from electrolytic hydrogen using nuclear power and nitrogen from air; and hydrazine, another potentially attractive fuel and considered synthetic because it can be made from electrolytic hydrogen and air.

Finally, there is wind power, which seems an almost bizarre and antiquated means to suggest for modern-day ship propulsion, but which is being very seriously considered. The economics resulting from high oil fuel prices now make it a viable proposition when considering that some routes are more than suited to sail, although ships can be designed to suit given routes. Already Japan has built the world's first twin-sail tanker *Shin Atiku Maru*, which is a 1,600 dwt vessel with two rigid sails consisting of thin steel frames carrying sailcloth, and has followed this with another similar vessel. Encouraged by the buoyant cruise liner market and the worldwide need for economic fuel propulsion, Wartsila in 1981 proposed a 110-passenger sail-powered cruise liner for which it can foresee a future.

Looking at unusual materials for ship construction, one that has a long history but is not too obvious to the layman, is concrete. The earliest concrete vessel dates from 1848. During the World War 1 period large concrete ocean-going vessels were built, thus demonstrating the feasibility of this material as a hull material. One such ship was the American vessel *Selma* (1922), the largest ever built at that time. In World War 2 a certain amount of concrete ships and floating structures were again built, including the unique Mulberry harbour pontoon complex used for the Normandy landings.

Two types of concrete are considered for marine use: reinforced concrete and ferrocement, which is a special form. The former has limited marine usage while the latter is already well established. Prestressed concrete is another consideration and German engineers first applied prestressing techniques in 1943. It seems that as sizes grow, more use will be made of prestressing techniques. Considering how large concrete ships can be expected to grow, approval was given by Lloyd's Register of Shipping in 1977 to the concept of a 128,000m LNG carrier to be built of post-tensioned and reinforced concrete.

Special Purpose Ships

The cable ship performs very specialised marine work and has an unusual history. Early engineers had to overcome the physics and electrical processes in laying cable in water and eventually, a successful transatlantic telegraph cable was laid in 1858. But is was not until 1956 that the first transatlantic telephone cable was completed. The earliest British cable ship was the *Monarch*, which was a paddle steamer, while the *Great Eastern* made an important contribution to this field as a cable layer. In 1916 the *Lord Kelvin* was built, being the first to establish a trend for working off the bow for all cable work. From such early vessels cable ships have evolved into a specialised class of ships coming under three main sub-categories: the repair ship, a combination repair/lay ship and a combination high speed lay/repair ship.

Among today's major cable ships are the British

British Telecom International's cable ship *Monarch* (*above*) was designed to include a number of features to improve cable handling, sea kindliness and station keeping. Built by Robb Caledon Shipbuilders Ltd, this 4,651-tonne vessel has an unmanned submersible (*below*) the *Seadog*, which swims and crawls along the seabed under remote control. Its prime function is to bury submarine cables to protect them from damage.   *British Telecom*

Monarch and the Japanese *Tsugaru Maru*, coming under the repair ship category, while combined repair and layer ships are represented by the Russian *Ingul* and Japanese *Kuroshio Maru*. The final category is best represented by the *Long Lines*.

Yet another special purpose ship is the icebreaker. Many vessels have been built for traversing through ice, including passenger ships, tugs, fishing vessels, etc. Some examples are the passenger cruiser *Song of Norway*, the car/passenger ferry *Finnjet*, and the first icebreaking bulk carrier *Thuleland*. Such vessels have strengthened scantlings, especially at the bow, which are approved by Lloyd's Register of Shipping or one of the other major classification societies. The Russians are very interested in icebreaking transport ships and could introduce 150,000 dwt cargo-carrying vessels in the future. Their Arctic fleet will acquire a series of five Finnish-built ships in 1982-83, while under a Five Year Plan a nuclear-powered lighter carrier will become the biggest dry cargo vessel with high ice capability. One shipyard that specialises in this form of construction is Wartsila of Finland, which has an existing ice model basin and one that was under construction in 1981 and completed in 1983. It is reckoned to be the largest of its kind.

An interesting sideline to icebreaking activities is the Russian dredger *Yogland* which is able to carry out dredging when in icy waters, thus enabling it to work all the year round — an important consideration in Russian waters.

The pure icebreaker has as its major task the job of making a passage through ice for other ships, as well as escorting them through such waters and performing secondary duties. When ice conditions are too thick for continuous operations it may have to resort to ramming. To obtain some idea of the thickness of ice such vessels can tackle, the US Coastguard icebreaker *Polar Star*, commissioned in 1976 and the first to be built for that service in more than 20 years, was estimated to be able to cut ice 6.4m thick by ramming. The vessel was the most powerful US icebreaker built up to that time. Another coastguard vessel recently built is the Canadian Arctic icebreaker CCGS *Pierre Radisson*, which joined the Canadian fleet in 1978 and was its first Arctic icebreaker since the late 1960s. An icebreaker landmark occurred when the Soviet nuclear-powered icebreaker *Arktika* reached the North Pole on 17 August 1977.

There is a Canadian design for an icebreaker to operate in the Beaufort Sea and North-West Passage, with a capability to cut through ice up to 2.4m at 3kts and by ramming to negotiate ice up to 8.7m.

Lastly, one other special purpose vessel is the research ship. This type of vessel performs a variety of functions, depending on the areas of research that it has been built for. Two of the weirdest looking vessels of this type are involved in space research and come under Russia's Academy of Sciences. The first is the flagship of the Academy's space service research fleet and is the 45,000 dwt *Kosmonavt Yuriy Gagarin*, built in 1971. It is the world's largest research vessel and has four parabolic aerial reflectors of 12-25m diameter, weighing nearly 1,000 tons in all, straddling its length in chimney stack fashion. Another strange marine beast — also belonging to Russia's space fleet — is the *Kosmanovt Vladimar Komarov*, whose three

The Japanese meteorological observation ships *Keifu Maru*, with 'golf ball' toppings to protect aerial reflectors from the elements. *IHI*

The IHI-built *Seiko Maru*, the world's first super-automated tanker, 138,000 dwt.   *IHI*

'mysterious' spheres surmounting its superstructure look like giant golf balls. Their real — and innocuous — purpose is to protect aerial reflectors against the elements. One other vessel with golf ball toppings is Japan's meteorological observation ship *Reifu Maru*.

Catamarans

In conclusion, vessels of unconventional design are now considered, and probably the most prominent and promising of these are the catamaran-type vessels. The word 'catamaran' comes from *katu-maran*, which means 'tied logs' in the Tamil language of South India. In Japanese it is translated *sadosen*, written in three characters meaning twin-hull ship, which is exactly what a catamaran is. In the mid-17th century Sir William Petty became interested in 'Double Bodeyed Shippes' as he called them, then later, in 1850, an iron catamaran — the *Gemini* — was built on the River Thames. Conventional catamaran ships have hull sec-

tions similar to a monohull ship, a large deck area, high stability and outstanding manoeuvrability. Since World War 2 technology in twin-hulled vessels has advanced rapidly and in the forefront of these efforts has been the United States and Japan.

A further stage in catamaran development was the semi-submersible concept, which has been variously known as the semi-submersible catamaran, the low waterplane catamaran, small waterplane area twin-hull ship, TRISEC and S^3. The first step in the development of such vessels can reasonably be placed with the hybrid catamaran, of which the 1,400-tonne workboat *Duplus* is a good example. The principle of semi-submersible catamaran vessels is to site the hull buoyancy fully below the waterline and the advantages obtained include the provision of a steady platform and the ability to maintain speed in bad sea conditions. Basically, the design consists of two torpedo-like hulls supporting a platform above the surface by means of streamlined struts. A number of SSC vessels have been built in the past decade or so, one example being the Japanese SSC passenger vessel built in 1979, having an aluminium alloy hull and a capacity for 446 passengers.

A catamaran-type vessel built by IHI, the work boat *Sokai*.   *IHI*